"We're Kin to WHO!!!??"

A Genealogical Research Guide to Some Early Families of Southampton and Isle of Wight Counties in Virginia and Surrounding Counties

Narratives and Research

by

Joe H. Drake

Heritage Books
2025

HERITAGE BOOKS

AN IMPRINT OF HERITAGE BOOKS, INC.

Books, CDs, and more—Worldwide

For our listing of thousands of titles see our website
at
www.HeritageBooks.com

Published 2025 by
HERITAGE BOOKS, INC.
Publishing Division
5810 Ruatan Street
Berwyn Heights, MD 20740

International Standard Book Number
Paperbound: 978-0-7884-5054-9

Dedicated

To

All Who Came Before

May We Always Remember

And

To Those Yet To Come

May You Never Forget

Table of Contents

	Frequently Encountered Abbreviations	vii
	Acknowledgements	ix
	Introduction	xi
Chapter I:	The Beginning	1
Chapter II:	Random Thoughts and Observations	7
Chapter III:	Paternity Suit Proceedings Against Hugo Grant, Age 103	15
Chapter IV:	Remembrances of Hugo	19
Chapter V:	The Founding and Founders of Barnes Methodist Church	27
Chapter VI:	And the Spirit Moved Him	39
Chapter VII:	Jacob Barnes of Southampton County, Virginia, Edgecombe, Northampton, and Pitt Counties, North Carolina	43
Chapter VIII:	The Search for Nathan Britt(Brett) and the Discovery	55
Chapter IX:	The Ancestors of John Henry Gurley Drake	59
Chapter X:	Family Shorts	71
Chapter XI:	Respectful Disagreement	79
Chapter XII:	Finding the Parents of Susan Edwards	85
Chapter XIII:	The Kitchen Family by Ulysses P. Joyner, Jr. (Pete)	87
Chapter XIV:	The Sermon	93
Chapter XV:	Rendezvous With History	95
Chapter XVI:	Final Thoughts	109
	Bibliography	113
	Index	117

Frequently Encountered Abbreviations

Abt – About or circa (may also be lower case)

B – Born (may also be lower case)

C – Circa, or about or around (may also be lower case)

CED – Charles Edward Francis Drake

CSA – Confederate States of America

Cty. – County

D – died (may also be lower case)

DB – Deed Book

Hert – Hertford

IoW – Isle of Wight

MB – Marriage Book

MR – Marriage Register

MVNN – Margaret Vann Ness Nelson

NC – North Carolina

NGSQ – National Genealogy Society Quarterly

Nhptn - Northampton

Shpton - Southampton

VA or Va - Virginia

WB – Will Book

Acknowledgement

First and foremost, I need to thank my editor, best friend, and wife of nearly fifty years, Linda Tomlin Drake. Without her help this work would not exist……but don't blame her for that, I made her do it. And I need to thank my grandson Carson Justin Drake to whom I showed the title page and he suggested I capitalize the word WHO, and add a couple of more question marks, and exclamation points. It works for me.

I have distant cousins who are/were very, very good at narrative and they have helped me a lot over the years with my research and to whom I would be remiss if I did not acknowledge their help and guidance: Ulysses "Pete" Joyner, a cousin on the Brett side of our family and author of "Joyner of Southampton" and "They Crossed the Blackwater" and Paul Drake, a cousin on the Drake side and author of "Now in Our Fourth Century", "You Ought to Write That Down" and "What Did They Mean By That? A Dictionary of Historical and Genealogical Terms Old and New". Both of these gentlemen have now passed away. They are greatly missed.

And, of course, Charles E. F. Drake, author of "Origins of the Drake Family of Isle of Wight County, Virginia" (a National Genealogical Society Quarterly Magazine article) and "The Drake Family of Washington County, Georgia". Years ago, I shudder to think of how many, Charles and I were conversing via email lamenting the fact that the Drakes, with all the many Richards, Johns, Thomases, and Barnabies, seemed impossible to tell who was who and when and where. So we embarked upon an ambitious project to find and sort all the Drakes of Isle of Wight and Southampton. The theory was that, to be sure you had the right Drake, you had to have them all. It took us between three and four years, but I believe we have identified and sorted every Drake for which there was a record in the courthouse in these counties from 1659 to 1850.

Gratitude is due Frank S. Walker: Dairyman farmer, lawyer, historical tour guide, descendant of Thomas Jefferson, kindred spirit, and author of several books on the history of Orange County, Virginia, but most of all friend. Frank's encouragement and willingness to critique my work have been of great value. Frank, you did not have to be so kind, but you were.

Many others have contributed to the information found here. They are too numerous to mention individually, but one can find their contributions in the footnotes and sources or they have been incorporated in the texts.

Thanks to All

Joe H. Drake

Feb. 2025

HEY THERE!!

CAN YOU SPARE A MINUTE?

Introduction

Thank you. Thank you for taking the time to read this. I will try to make it worth your time. I have read probably thousands of books in my life and, to be honest, I can't recall ever reading an introduction. If I did, they didn't seem to make much of an impression, so let us see if this introduction can be a bit different.

You are sitting in front of the roll-top desk of your mind. Let us hope both, mind and desk, are open. You are looking at the "pigeon holes" of the desk wondering in which hole this book and reference work should be. There is the CD. It has an index with one hundred forty pages of names (13,233 at last count) and page numbers. The CD has well over a thousand family pages comprising one to eight pages each. This is easy. The CD goes in the pigeon hole marked "reference work."

And then there is the narrative work. It is a book containing 16 chapters and, quite frankly, it is all over the place in terms of content. No one pigeon hole will hold it. Yes it has some of the standard genealogical works, written in the standard genealogical style complete with footnotes and sources. All five of those chapters were adapted from articles written over the years for various historical societies' publications and/or websites. These can be put in the hole marked genealogical works. Relatively simple to classify these chapters.

But then we take a closer look at the first two chapters and things are not so simple anymore. The first two chapters were intended to convey the character of the reference material, and they do. But that information is wedged between historical stories and antidotes – some of which are humorous, some not so much. And then there is an attempt to apply statistical analysis to the reference material, or some selected parts of it. This will probably present an aspect to genealogy that most people probably never considered and it can be a bit revealing. Statistical analysis: it is not nearly as boring as it sounds on the surface. At the time you are reading it, you probably will not realize that what you just read was statistical analysis. We leave those chapters lying on the desk for now because we have no idea in which pigeon hole they should be.

And then there is the true story of a 103 year old man who finds himself in a paternity suit. This is a two chapter character study that covers more than a century. The chapters include glimpses into the Depression, prison life in the forties, and farm life of the 1960's. It is a remarkable story of a simple man. What do these two chapters have to do with genealogy? Not a damn thing – but they form part of the family history of all who knew the man. We will pigeon hole this in the character study slot for the time being.

There is a chapter in which the conclusions of a genealogy icon are respectfully challenged – and the word respectfully cannot be emphasized enough. This is a story of relentless research, the careful taking of notes, and how often the research of one family can find its way into the research of another. Put this one in the pigeon hole labeled "continuing research."

Family Shorts is an often light-hearted collection of tales and antidotes. The chapter is included just to entertain the reader. It has some family history. It has some tales that are curiosities, mostly involving mules of all things. This one goes in the just for fun hole.

The chapter entitled "Finding the Parents of Susan Edwards" is a case study in the search for ancestors. It goes through the steps required to build a case for clear and convincing evidence and the establishment of probable parents. This chapter we slide into the pigeon hole labeled genealogical how to.

What could be better than a story about inspiration? How about a story of inspiration and moonshine? The story has some genealogical and historical elements but is primarily about a man, his still, and his inspiration. It is different. You will find this chapter in the "not quite sure what it is but it is different" slot of our roll-top desk.

All thirteen thousand plus people of this reference work did not exist in a vacuum. They interacted with the world around them and the world interacted with them. All of them had an effect on history, some more than others. The chapter "Rendezvous with History" examines history prior to 1865 and the roles some of the subject people played in it or as noted in the sub-title "where micro-history collides with macro-history."

"The Sermon" and "Final Thoughts" finish out the book. "The Sermon" attempts to make the case that we all should try to record some aspects of our family history for those who will come after us. This book would have been far more interesting had some of the subjects left some of their thoughts and experiences. The people researched in this research guide span a time period of over four hundred years and they left us – only us. As far as any written recordings, we have nothing. There are a few more antidotes in the Final Thoughts, but it basically just ends the work. Pigeon hole these as ending chapters.

And there you have it. You have now been introduced to the book. Thank you for reading this. I probably would not have done it. I only hope you received some enjoyment from this introduction. And now - on to the book.

YOU REALLY SHOULD READ THIS BEFORE YOU START

IN THE BEGINNING

KEEP IT LIGHT
To most researchers, family history and genealogy is serious, heavy stuff. It doesn't have to be. This author takes his research very seriously, but the telling of the stories of our research subjects....Those tales should be a friendly conversation the author has with the readers, not an authoritative lecture. So as you read this narrative section of the book, remember I'm talking with you, not preaching at you.

ERRORS
All works of genealogy contain errors. The more comprehensive the work, the more errors it contains. This work has errors - probably a lot of errors. I don't know where they are. If I did, I would fix them. So, when the people who delight in finding the errors and faults of others say "look what you did, you were wrong!!" , I can say "yeah, well, **I told you so!**" But I won't. I'll politely say thank you, fix my mistake, and move on.

I, ME, MY
I intensely dislike writing in the first person, but there are times when it can not be avoided. This introduction is one of those times. I am convinced the only one who can rightfully write in the first person was Adam (had he had an alphabet).

ACKNOWLEDGEMENT
I intensely dislike writing narrative. By background and education, I am more attuned to technical writing (which kept me off academic probation in college) where one takes a long narrative about a machine or industrial process and condenses it to the bare facts needed to convey the message and presents those facts in an easy to understand format.

But I have distant cousins who are/were very, very good at narrative and they have helped me a lot over the years with my research and to whom I would be remiss if I did not acknowledge their help and guidance: Ulysses "Pete" Joyner, a cousin on the Brett side of our family and author of "*Joyner of Southampton*" and "*They Crossed the Blackwater*" and Paul Drake, a cousin on the Drake side and author of "*Now in Our Fourth Century*", "*You Ought to Write That Down*" and "*What Did They Mean By That? A Dictionary of Historical and Genealogical Terms Old and New*".

And, of course, Charles E. F. Drake, author of "*Origins of the Drake Family of Isle of Wight County, Virginia*" (a National Genealogical Society Quarterly Magazine article) and "*The Drake Family of Washington County, Georgia*". Years ago, I shudder to think of how many, Charles and I were conversing via email lamenting the fact that the Drakes, with all the many Richards, Johns, Thomases, and Barnabies, seemed impossible to tell who was who and when and where. So we embarked upon an ambitious project to find and sort all the Drakes of Isle of Wight and Southampton. The theory was that, to be sure you had the right Drake, you had to have them all. It took us between three and four years, but I believe we have identified and sorted every Drake for which there was a record in the courthouse in these counties from 1659 to 1850.

Many others have contributed to the information found here. They are too numerous to mention individually, but one can find their contributions in the footnotes and sources.

Now, the publishers thought I should move this acknowledgement to a separate page at the beginning of the book. And they are probably right. However only a few people ever read the acknowledgement page and it was important to me that these three get some recognition. I doubt you read it, but there is an acknowledgement page at the front just as conventional wisdom says there should be. The sensibilities of both parties have now been satisfied.

WHAT THIS IS

This was going to be called an encyclopedia of some Southampton/Isle of Wight families, but it was realized that this work is not nearly authoritative enough nor formatted properly to be called an encyclopedia. So this can more properly be called a research guide. The reader/researcher of this work is encouraged to check the sources for themselves and reach their own conclusions.

The people are loosely arranged alphabetically by family name, so the table of contents is also the index. With the number of people researched, I got lazy. Rather than type a whole new page for each family, a family group sheet was printed using "*Family Tree Maker*". That usually means most people are listed at least twice: once with their parents' family group sheet and then with their own family group sheet.

BY THE NUMBERS

The number of people included are well over thirteen thousand, give or take a couple of hundred. The number of surnames exceeds 980. The earliest birth date is estimated at about 1550. The median birth year is 1781, which means half of the people in the data base were born prior to 1781 and half after that time.

The true value of this work lies in the fact that over 80% of the individuals researched were born prior to 1850. For those new to genealogical research, this is important because the census of 1850 was the first in which each person within a household is listed by name and age. In any prior census only the name of the head of household was listed. For the most part, research from 1850 and forward in time is considerably easier than before 1850.

As a loose rule, people born after 1850 or who had left Southampton and the surrounding counties, tended not to be researched to the same extent as those in Southampton and Isle of Wight before 1850.

WHO'S HERE

When I was a lad of 13 or 14, some fifty-five plus years ago, I thought I might be a descendent of Sir Francis Drake, the great English admiral. I was not nor was anyone else. The old pirate died childless, or as the genealogists like to say, "without issue". So if Sir Francis was not family, who was? This started a quest to find who was in my family - surely one of them had to be interesting. The concepts of family history or genealogy had nothing to do with it. I only wanted to see to whom I might be kin.

Everyone in this research guide is family, or my wife's family (whose research I shamelessly plagiarized), or family of family if not direct kin, and/or the family of in-laws. This being the case, the surnamed Drake family is well represented with about 630+ individuals, the Brett family 450+, Bryant 375+, Barnes 361+. The second largest group is the unknown wives, as in a last will and testament - "and to my loving wife, Ann, I leave..." Ann who? There are as yet over 450 wives whose given names are known but their maiden names are yet to be discovered. (As an aside, old wills can be really interesting. I always look to see which favored child inherited the brandy still. Most antebellum wills listed a still.)

SOURCES AND STANDARDS OF PROOF

Paul Drake, JD, being the attorney he was, liked to think of genealogical proof in terms of the three legal standards of proof. Those are evidentiary proof beyond a reasonable doubt, evidentiary proof that is both clear and convincing, and proof by a preponderance of the evidence. Now, all of this is really subjective: what may be proof beyond a reasonable doubt to one may be only a preponderance of evidence to another.

Among the thousands of people and hundreds of family names in this work, you will find all of the above. It is up to each researcher to evaluate the quality of the source and determine the likelihood that the families are grouped properly.

In general the courthouse records, wills, deeds, case records, and tax lists are solid evidence - the only question being was the information interpreted and applied properly.

Note: In this work, when the source for a death date is given as a will, the date is the date the will was ordered recorded. The actual date of death would normally have been within thirty days or so prior to the recording date.

Census records are useful, but beware of how names are spelled. That can lead the researcher astray. (see "Hooked on *Fonics*" below)

Cemetery records: If one were to really think about it, grave markers are only hearsay - with the person most qualified to judge the accuracy of the information lying under the marker. That being said, cemetery records are usually very accurate.

Books are usually reliable but, in the final analysis, are only as good as the author's research.

In this work, you will encounter sources listed as from someone's genealogical notes.
Only those people known to be quality, trusted researchers are quoted. They could be wrong, but usually they are not.

Oral histories are used. These are from sources known to have first-hand knowledge of what they speak or to have gained knowledge from someone who had first-hand knowledge. Only those oral histories believed to be unimpeachable are used.

There are some few entries based on message board postings and online family tree postings. These may be reliable or not. Beware! They should be looked upon as a starting point for something to be verified.

And then there are the entries and information that have no sources at all. These are generally from sources of which the reliability is unknown and untested (in many cases, if not most, from really good sources that I forgot to write down in my earlier research). All such information should be used with caution until verified. Such information was included so it would not be lost until proven or documented. This information is thought to be correct, but still needs better proof.

GEOGRAPGHY, POLITICS, AND POOR PEOPLE

Occasionally, I am amused when I read a message board post or an email from someone who asserts that his/her ancestor was the son of a rich person back in England, a person of societal consequence who came to Isle of Wight/Southampton to expand influence and fortune, or was some illegitimate child of royalty who was given a land grant (or royal patent) in this neck of the woods. Southampton County, Virginia, today is 60% wooded. A large part of that forest land is wetlands or swamp, and this is after 300 - 350 years of clearing and draining. A malarial swamp is not the most advantageous place to seek a fortune. But, if you were an indentured servant recently freed and entitled to a 50 acre patent of land (100 if your wife is also a former indentured servant) on which to build a home, clear a few acres and plant a crop (conditions of a patent), the area had advantages.

Judging from my research, the people of early Isle of Wight/Southampton were in large part former indentured servants and some Quakers. The former servants were poor, illiterate, and naturally distrustful of government and authority. The Quakers, not being members of the government-sponsored Church of England, had been persecuted for their religious beliefs for years. Both of these groups were very happy to be as far from the colonial authorities as they could get, that being Jamestown on the *other* side of the James River. (Some would be active participants of Bacon's Rebellion in 1676, five of whom are known to be in this work and perhaps three others if their estimated birth years are off by ten). So if you are looking for your long lost **rich** ancestor, this isn't the place. For many of these early settlers, when you read the inventories of their estates, all of their worldly possessions can be listed on a single sheet of a legal pad - single column.

There were others (a bit better off) who held multiple headrights entitling them to larger tracts of lands which would have been available in the area, but they seem to be a minority of the settlers.

Just as a point of historical fact, one of the very first settlers **was** a rich merchant, a man by the name of Bennett. About 1620, he sent his brother over to Isle of Wight to carve out a fortune. But all this is balanced by the fact that his brother brought 120 poor people with him (that's 120 headrights at 50 acres each or 6,000 acres). By 1624, after the 1622 Good Friday Indian massacre, most of those people including the brother Bennett would be dead.

In the "Muster of 1624", there were only 53 people on the south side of the James River,
in what would be Isle of Wight and the area that would become Surry County, living along the River. By 1635, that number had increased to 522 individuals in a county of about 965 square miles or one person every two square miles. The next comprehensive count was in 1658 in which 2019 people were enumerated - about two persons per square mile. (That's a bit misleading: the 605 square miles of Isle of Wight, which would become Southampton, south of the Blackwater River, supposedly was not open to settlement. It was reserved for the native tribes; however, many whites were building homesteads in the area. In 1700, the claims of the natives were ignored and the area was officially open to settlement.)

To be sure, early records from this period are hard to find and difficult to read at times. The good news is there are fewer people to whom these records apply. This research guide has <u>at least</u> 110 people thought to have been in Isle of Wight County in 1658 (some of whom would have been children). Those 110 souls represent about 5% of the total population of the county at that time.

HOOKED ON *FONICS*

Very few people, from the early 1600's until just before the Civil War, were literate - the earlier the date, the fewer the number of people who could read or write. The consequence was, when our early ancestors did have to interact with the local government, very few knew how to spell their names. The result being the clerks, scribes, or clergy would spell their names phonetically. This led to people in the same family having their family names spelled several ways. A few personal examples:

My third great-grandfather on his marriage bond (1804) had his name spelled BRITT at the top of the bond and BRETT at the bottom. He signed with an X.

In a family Bible that was found in my great-grandfather's house, my great-great-grandfather had his name spelled Cowan, his father Cowand, and HIS father Cowwins. This all was on the same page, but in three different hands.

There is a tale, genuine family lore, of two Brett/Britt brothers whose wives detested each other. So one insisted that the family name be spelled Brett; the other demanded Britt so they could claim no connection. The brothers, not being able to write, probably didn't know the difference, probably didn't care, and probably figured it best just to stay out of it.

For the sake of simplicity, expediency, and the author's sanity, only the most common spelling used in this general area is used to denote a family in this work. Some, but perhaps not all, of these names are most-used name variations:

Allen - Allin, Allon
Applewhite - Applewait
Barrow - Borrow, Barrows
Blount - Blont, Blunt
Boddie - Body, Bodye
Booth - Boothe
Braswell - Bracewell
Brett - Britt, Breet, Brat, Breatt
Bryant - Briand, Bryan, Brian
Bynum - Byrum
Caroon -Caroone
Coggins - Coggin, Cogin
Cowan - Cowand, Cowwins
Edmonds - Edmunds
Gale - Guil, Gail
Holloman – Holliman, Hollaman
Joyner - Joiner
Lewis - Louis
Newsom - Newsoms, Newsome
Rea - Rae, Ray, Wray
Thorpe - Thorp, Tharp, Tharpe
Anderson - Andersen
Bailey - Baylie
Beale - Beal, Beel
Blythe - Bly
Boon - Boone
Bowles - Bowels
Bressie – Brasey, Bracy
Browne - Brown
Burgess - Burges
Campion - Champion
Chitty - Chittee
Cook - Cooke, Cocke
Doyal - Doyel, Doyle, Doyell, Dawel
Eley - Ely
Hayes - Hase, Haies
Johnson - Johnston
Kitchen - Kenchen
Maget - Magette
Philips - Phillips
Revel - Revil, Reville

THE DIMINISHING GENE POOL OF THE THREE MILE PER HOUR WORLD
Some good advice given years ago: when you are stuck trying to figure out who an ancestor married, look across the creek, not across the state. As one examines these early Isle of Wight/Southampton people, patterns arise in which a relatively small number of surnames within a local area keep intermarrying. This is understandable given our ancestors of the 17th, 18th and 19th centuries lived in a "three mile an hour" world. It would take a young person two hours to go five to six miles: a long way and a long time to youths with courting on their minds. So the number of families within a given area was limited and the distance to be covered in a given time was limited with the result of the same families intermarrying. At some point the researcher using this work will realize "these families sure do overlap a lot". This is the explanation.

Also, when researching those in early Southampton County, *beware the Nottoway.* From Courtland to the North Carolina line and beyond, the Nottoway River cannot be forded. If one did not have a boat, the use of one of the two known ferries, or the ability to swim, one did not cross the river. Early in the 19th century Cypress Bridge was built about five miles down stream from Courtland (Jerusalem), but that still left 10 to 15 miles of river to Carolina that cannot be forded. This tends to limit social contact.

A DIFFERENT PERSPECTIVE

At the start of this chapter, I noted three outstanding authors who have helped a great deal over the years. Among them are two lawyers and a cardiologist – men of letters and medicine. A great deal of the genealogical works is by professional genealogists, lawyers, doctors, historians. and college professors; generally, people of letters. Your humble author's training is in industrial technology and business administration – disciplines of numbers and math rather than letters. You will see evidence in the next chapter where an attempt at statistical analysis is applied to genealogy. (Industrial technology: think of it as engineering light. Mechanical engineers go into great detail of all things mechanical, electrical engineers into great detail in the electrical stuff, and so on with the different fields of study. Industrial technology hits the high points of all various engineering endeavors without too much detail in any one of them – the perfect study for those of us engineer wannabes with some limited attention spans.)

You can always tell a letters person. When you send them an example of your work, they notice all the misspelling, grammatical, and punctuation errors first and then get to the content. Drives us numbers people crazy.

THE END OF THE BEGINNING

For all those new to family research, I hope this guide will be of use. Most importantly, have fun in your search and discoveries. For the serious genealogists who may think this introduction a bit flippant - get a life.

To all those family historians who have preceded us – thank you. And to all those today and yet to come -- yeah, well, **I told you so.**

Joe H. Drake
From the edge of the *Great Cypress Swamp* (AKA Darden Mill Run) in
the area of rural free delivery of Newsoms, Southampton County, Commonwealth of Virginia.
bmc2@mindspring.com

AS ODD AS IT SOUNDS A STILL IS A MOVABLE

Random Thoughts and Observations

As odd as it sounds, a still does not stay still; it is a movable. In old wills, the estates were divided into real estate and movables - movables being anything not physically attached to the land, like a house or barn. All other property could be moved, thus the name "movables". So a still might not necessarily be still.

And speaking of stills and wills:

Most old wills follow a pattern: the soul of the dearly departed was left to God, provisions made for the widow (if a male deceased), the land devised, and then either how the slaves were to be proportioned or - the moment all were awaiting - who received the brandy still. (As an anticlimax, usually it was then discovered who got which feather bed with its furniture, then the other items: hogs, cows, sheep, the contents of the smokehouse.)

If two of his children might be in a state of discord, the deceased in his will might leave the still cap to one and the worm to the other, thus forcing them to work together. Thus brandy was used as a mender of family relationships.

{For the still illiterate, the cap was the part of the still shaped like an upside down funnel. It fit over the boiling pot which contained the "mash" if making whiskey or wine if making brandy. The worm was often a length of cork screw shaped tubing which acted as the condenser that fit into the top of the cap. If you do not understand, you are still – still illiterate.}

Brandy - grief counselor and sales aid:

Judging from several 18th century estate accountings, the standard amount of brandy purchased for a funeral was two gallons. An estate auction sale usually required three gallons of brandy. The accounts do not state if the potent potable was administered before, during, or after the proceedings.

Brandy, Hams, and Railroads

Brandy became one of Southampton County's biggest cash crops. Another was salt-cured smoked hams and pork middling (bacon). Around 1835/36, the railroad made its way into the county (afore said mentioned, as they would say in a deed) on its way to Roanoke Rapids, NC. Construction slowed when it reached the Nottoway River. At that point the little community of Delaware sprang up. At the present time, nearly two hundred years later, it is not known if it was a sort of antique amusement park and/or picnic grounds or just a place to fish while the train turned around for the return trip to Norfolk, Portsmouth, and Suffolk. Whatever it was, people from the urban areas to the east would make a day trip by riding the train to Delaware, partake of the brandy and ham that was sold there, and then ride back to the big towns hopefully happier than when they first left.

Mary, the Merry Widow

When one Benjamin Lewis died about 1790, his will directed that his wife, widow, and relic Mary should have full use of his personal estate during her life. At her death the estate was to be divided between "all my children". Mary passed away around late 1795-early 1796 and on 1 April 1796, appropriately April Fool's Day, the seven children (Zebulon, Benjamin, Elizabeth, Fanny, Nanny, Sarah, and Rebeccah) divided the estate. It was determined at that time that each sibling was to receive, among other things, **56 gallons** of brandy. That is a total of 392 gallons of the spirit or, if bottled, 1,960 fifths (which would probably stock every ABC store in the Commonwealth of Virginia). It would seem that Mary had been really busy.

Oddly enough, it was not recorded which of the seven children got the still. It was probably worn out.

Final Brandy Tale (tah-dah)

The author's grandfather, Rufus E. Drake, was one of the younger of the second batch of children born to Thomas Harrison Drake. Thomas was a Civil War veteran whose eleven children were spread over a time period of 33 years. Five foot-eight with reddish brown hair and blue eyes, Thomas started growing a beard when he left for the war toward the last of April, 1861, that he would not shave until the day he died in 1913. Granddaddy Rufus always said that none of the eleven children ever saw the face of their father.

Thomas Harrison Drake's farm, where these words are being written, was dotted with apple trees. The crops of corn and cotton were grown between the trees. There was a big old barn on the farm where he stored cider, vinegar, and the base stock of apple wine for his brandy. Circa 1895, one Joe S. Bryant ventured out to this barn with its many barrels to speak to Thomas about marrying his daughter, Betty.

Picture in your mind a nervous young man facing the gnarled, bewhiskered old veteran of Cold Harbor, the Petersburg trenches, Fort Fisher, and Bentonville about to ask him to part with one of his daughters. Thomas had to have a very good idea of what Uncle Joe wanted and he probably knew and could see how nervous and apprehensive the poor young man was. One might think that Thomas, perhaps, would show a bit of empathy for the young man, right? Hell, no. Before Joe Bryant could say a word, Thomas handed him a dipper and asked him which barrel would make the best brandy. After sampling several, Uncle Joe picked one. To which Thomas replied "Yep, just as I thought. Don't know a damn thing about it."
(Well, it sounded funny when Granddaddy told it.)

"It's amazing how the life of one person can touch the lives of so many others"
Clarence Oddbody, AS II (angel second class)
"It's a Wonderful Life" Republic pictures, 1946

Evolution

Like most works of genealogy, this work began with the author only wanting to find his direct ancestors. Somewhere along the way, the siblings of those direct ancestors were added, then the children of the siblings, then the in-laws to all of the above, then the families of the in-laws and on and on. While researching the ancestors, siblings, in-laws, and all the families thereof, piles and piles of people and interesting facts were observed that would be noted just in case they might be needed one day. A great many of those notes have now found their way into this work and the number of those researched grew.

At some point it was realized that it was more fun and more of a challenge to work with the really old records, those being the records prior to 1850 when the change in the census made genealogical life much simpler. Then the realization set in that there were far fewer people to find and deal with - the records to people ratio was much closer. This simplified the work: while over all time there might be a dozen John Does, in just the colonial era, there might be only two or three or - better yet - only one.

And finally, because they were there and available, and because it had never been done, the author undertook the task of reading (scanning might would be a better word) all the documents from the clerk's office for the first 50 years of Southampton County - 1749 to 1800. Another reason for doing this was to find what he might have missed; as it turned out, he had missed over 2,000 people with family connections to those already found. (This took a long while: most of his free time for two years and, in retrospect, was probably a damn fool thing to do.)

If a person has the patience and the time to turn so many pages, they would find that each and every person in this work can be connected to all the others found in this work.

Thank you, Ken Brantley

As noted above, all the records for the first 50 years of Southampton County were read or perused. Although the author has spent countless hours in various courthouses for over a half century, especially the Southampton Courthouse in Courtland, going over so many records of Southampton would not have been possible without the efforts of Ken Brantley of the Brantley Association.

Several years ago, for the price of only a motel room, Ken photographed all the pages from all the record books of Southampton County from its inception in 1749 thru the year 1881. Quick, rough count yields over 40,000 pages photographed by Ken. All of these are available on-line at:

www.brantleyassociation.com/southampton_project/southampton_project_list.htm

Ken, your efforts are greatly appreciated. Now everyone rush to your computers, find the above link and hunt for errors in this work (they're there, don't know where, but they are).

Tales to Tell

There are over 13,000 names in this work, just faceless names on paper. But each of those names represented a living, loving, breathing individual. All of them have (note present tense) a story to be told. This work fails to even remotely begin to tell those stories. This work builds a skeleton of a family and, in a larger part, a societal framework that will hopefully help others tell the stories that have not been told here. If just a few of those tales are found and told, this work would have been worth the effort.

One Big Happy Family?

From the author's grandson to his earliest found ancestor, parts of sixteen generations have been found. These sixteen generations cover a time period of about 450 years. Most people have never thought about just how many persons of direct lineage we have the potential to research considering that many years and generations.

Consider the first (actually the latest) generation; that would be one person. Add his/her parents, two more people, and a cumulative total of three. Add the third generation, the grandparents, a total of four more persons bringing the cumulative total to seven. By the time you get to the 16th generation, that is the 13X great-grandparents, that generation has a potential total of (assuming no cousins marry) 32,768 people and an accumulation of 65,535 people over all.

Grandson has a lot of work and research left to do. But the good news, maybe, is that cousins do marry and drastically reduce these numbers.

What Are The Odds?

The parents of the author of this work are cousins. They have a common Bryant ancestor six generations back making them fourth cousins, meaning they share about 1.5% of their DNA. Both have roots deep into Southampton/Isle of Wight. When the author told his brother of this, his reply was "well, what are the odds of that happening?".

So let's see if we can come up with an approximation of those odds. Both the Drake and the Brett families can be traced back to 1660 Isle of Wight County and before. At that time, judging from the number of tithables, the number of families in the county would have been less than 500, probably about 450. In the twelve generations between the earliest known ancestors of the author's parents and their births, they each had a potential of over 4,000 chances (the cumulative number of ancestors over twelve generations) of an incidence of a common set of ancestors. So even if one or both of the parents of the author had half their ancestors come from outside the area, that still leaves 2,000 chances for a marriage between those 450 families of 1660 over the course of 280 years. What are the odds? For any one year, the odds are 1 in 65. So every 65 years there is probably an incidence of cousins marrying. Over 280 years the odds become 4 to 1 that cousins **will** marry and **that is if both parties have half their ancestors from out of the area - which did not happen.** The odds: nearly a mathematical certainty.

Southampton/Isle of Wight for about three centuries, from the first settlers until after WW II, was a semi-closed society in that people would be born and raised here and immigrate to other places but seldom did any new people come in. Such is the nature of an agricultural community. If you don't farm, you don't make a living. If you don't control enough land to earn a living farming, you have to leave. New people coming in did not control the land, ergo they could seldom earn a living so they did not stay.

If we go forward a generation, the author's wife also has deep roots to early Isle of Wight. Now the number of chances of common ancestors doubles with the new generation, and sure enough, there are common ancestors on both the Drake (back 12 generations) and the Brett (back 7 generations) sides of the family.

The author's son also married a local girl with deep roots in the area. Again the chances of interaction double with the new generation so one would expect there to be four sets of common ancestors. There are not four, but five sets of common ancestors.

Had there been no sets of common ancestors, that would have truly been a numerical aberration. So what are the odds?........... Nearly a mathematical certainty.

Ignorance may only be a temporary condition,
Stupidity is permanent.
Author known but modesty prevents him from being named.

This Might Explain a Lot

Granddaddy Rufus used to say "never talk bad about somebody 'cause you never know who they're kin to." It was previously postulated that Southampton/Isle of Wight was a semi-closed county with people migrating out, but few coming in. Judging by the tithables, when Southampton was formed in 1749, there were approximately 5,600 people in the new county: about 3800 whites and 1800 slaves and free blacks. This suggests approximately 640 family units. Scouring the land books, tax lists, and the list of freeholders yields 208 surnames in the new county. So, on average, each surname was represented by a bit over 3 family units. There certainly must be other family names that managed to avoid the various tax lists, but probably not many.

There were other family names earlier, but they either migrated to North Carolina or they stayed north of the Blackwater in Isle of Wright. As for Southampton, it would seem that from its very inception the families were well- mingled. A few new surnames would appear as new patents were granted, but the majority of the new patents issued in Southampton after 1749 went to the existing patentees or members of their families.

As for the 208 surnames found at the county's founding, all but three are represented in this work. Those missing are Dorby, Sundie, and Gwaltney. The first two are unfamiliar to the author. The Gwaltneys are a known family, but maybe they just don't like us!?

In the mid 18th century, if one was in Southampton and marrying someone from within the county, there was a good chance cousins were being married. Today, if you are from Southampton and are one of the 208 names on the list wedding another from the list, there is little doubt about it: you are marrying a cousin (probably a really, really distant cousin, but a cousin nevertheless). All these cousins getting wed.....might explain a lot!!

Granddaddy should have said “never talk bad about anybody” because they **are** kin to everyone.

The good news for the descendants of those who migrated from Southampton, when your research finally brings you back, you'll find a lot of family - real close together in a bunch....like bananas.

People Dating:

Having a birth date, even if it is estimated, is always good place to start with anyone in genealogy. All people in this work have a birth year. Most are estimated. As for setting dates, several loose rules applied.

People are on average born 30 to 35 years after their parents.
Husbands are, on average, 5 years older than their wives.
As a general rule, people had to be "of age", 21 or more, to witness a will or deed.
A parent named in a wedding bond usually indicated the bride or groom to be under the age of 21.
Orphans in the guardian accounts were not more than 21(and usually much less) from the date of the account.
A person listed on the tax list as a tithable was over the age of 16.

Note that in this work one will see brothers and sisters with the same estimated birth year. This is because the birth order is not known. The date given represents the best estimate of the middle of the range of births with some siblings born before the date and some after.

Duplicate References

Many duplicate references have been omitted. For example, if we know from John Doe's will the given name of his wife was Jane, we would gain very little by quoting one or more deeds by which John Doe and wife Jane transferred land to Jack Spratt et. al. A source from a last will and testament always takes precedence over everything else.

Following the Land

Although thousands, yes thousands, of deeds were read in researching this work, only those which gave some sort of relevant genealogical information are referenced. For those who feel all deeds should be explored and the land followed from person to person to insure nothing was missed, help yourself and good luck. This is a research guide, not an all-the-research-done-for-you work.

Witness Costs vs. Benefits

In this work, in fact in all the research leading to this work, witnesses were seldom recorded. Perhaps they should have been. On some occasions, it might have been helpful. The problem is/was that, while recording the names of witnesses to wills and deeds sometimes comes in handy (not very often but sometimes), it would have swelled the number of people for which there were notes from approximately 15,000 to more than 30,000. This number is far beyond the mental capabilities of the author. And again, this is a research guide, not an all-the-research-done-for-you work.

Which Way Did They Go???

While there are thousands of people in this work, only a comparatively few left wills, and there are no large number of administrations granted for those who might have died intestate. The obvious reason for this is that many of the people found in this research guide migrated to other parts of the country. We know of some who went to North Carolina: Hertford, Northampton, Edgecombe, Pitt, Wake, Nash and Johnston to name a few N.C. counties that had quite a number of people from Southampton/Isle of Wight to move there. Some wandered further south: South Carolina, Georgia and beyond. Some went west: Missouri, Ohio and beyond. The problem is, unless there is a will listing where they may be, a deed where a resident of elsewhere sells real estate in Southampton, or some latter-day family researcher from beyond finds his/her way back to the area and asks for help, we have no way of knowing who might have gone where.

But one thing is fairly certain. If they dropped off the tax lists and were not put in jail for it, they probably left.

"Nothing is foolproof because fools are so darn ingenious"
Author unknown

Body Count and No System is Perfect (Some Ain't Even Good)

The headright system was put in place to encourage immigration to Virginia (and later Maryland and some other colonies adopted a similar system). The plan was such that, when a person came to the colony, he or she was given a patent for 50 acres of land either at their arrival or at the end of their indenture. An additional patent for 50 acres was given to someone for each person for whom a passage to the colony was paid. A paid passage created a headright.

To perfect a patent, one had to prove the land inhabited by building some sort of abode, clearing an acre of land, and planting a crop - all this usually within a year. It made no difference how many acres were included in the patent and the person receiving the patent did not have to be the one occupying the land.

Simple system, right? What could possibly go wrong? Well............Some sea captains, English merchants and others would sell the headrights for people who never existed and/or claim they died at sea. Evidently, a person need only to board a ship to create the basis for a headright, not necessarily live to get here. It seems no one bothered to see that a headright was used only once. Captain John Upton of Isle of Wight (an officer in the militia who held several positions in the government of the colony) used the same name four times in three years to claim headrights. In fact he did this deed twice. An immigrant might find if he could check, and he couldn't because no records were being kept, that his headright might have existed in three or more counties of the colony at one time and used two or more years: headrights had no expiration date. Nobody was checking to see if the system was working properly as there was plenty of land and a King three thousand miles away wouldn't miss a few extra acres of his land being given away. The biggest of the defrauders seem to have been part of the elite, or the in-crowd.

In 1912, a fellow by the name of George Cabell Greer published a book "*Early Virginia Immigrants 1623 - 1666*". From the old patents, Mr. Greer tabulated who the early immigrants were, for whom a headright was claimed, who claimed and applied that headright to a patent, and where the patent thus issued was located. In 2011, Allen Price put this information in a digital form and made it available online. Mr. Greer had found more than 17,000 names of immigrants during this 43 year period with headrights claimed by approximately 7,000 individuals.

The author of this work separated the Warrasquinoke (which became Isle Of Wight County) and the Isle of Wight patents from the others. Seven hundred ninety-four of the 17,000 headrights were for Isle of Wight. Of these, 123 were repeat or multiple listings. Some 15.5% of the people for whom headrights were claimed were claimed more than once in Isle of Wight county (and perhaps in other counties as well). The two persons who abused the system the most were Captain John Upton and Justinian Cooper. During this period, Upton claimed 116 headrights from 67 individuals and Cooper claimed 75 headrights from 49 individuals. Between the two, Upton and Cooper had 75 of the 123 fraudulent headrights in Isle of Wight for the time period researched, or 61% of all of the the questionable headrights. In all, 88 men and 2 women received patents in Isle of Wight according to information extrapolated from Greer's work.

Eight others from Isle of Wight took unjust advantage of the system by using the same headright multiple times, duplicating immigrates' names 48 times. Eighty of the ninety patentees in the county seem to have abided by the rules.

Conclusion: The 17,000 immigrants for the period 1623-1666 are inflated by as much as 20% (perhaps even more). From a genealogical research standpoint, this creates a mess in that the researcher can not be sure of where an ancestor was indentured, or to whom, or when, or even if the name found is a real person or one created by fraud.

The True Meaning of Love

There is a bill of sale recorded in Southampton Deed Book 8 where, on 11 February 1796, Abraham Browne sells to Benjamin Drew a slave. This in and of itself is not unusual as there are lots of bills of sale for slaves recorded in the deed books as well as manumissions of slaves. What makes this bill of sale unique are the conditions attached to the sale. The sale has a time limit of 50 years (which would probably make it an indenture rather than a sale). Benjamin Drew has a slave, Aggie. If she or her two children are sold, the bill of sale is null and void. At the death of Benjamin Drew, the bill of sale is null and void. And for this sale, Abraham Browne receives six shillings (about 4% of the average value of a slave at that time).

Abraham Browne, free Negro, is selling himself into slavery and giving up his freedom. Aggie and her two children are Abraham Browne's wife and children.

Be Careful of What You Wish. You Might Just Get It

Wright Allen had problems. It seems that a fraudulent note, IOU, bond had turned up by which he, Wright Allen, had allegedly obtained money under false pretends. Wright Allen did not want to repay the money and he certainly did not want to go to jail. What was he to do? It seemed to Wright Allen that, if there were no note, IOU, bond, there would be no evidence of his criminal activity. No evidence – no conviction. Wright Allen would be free and would get to keep the money. Sure that the evidence was in the Hertford County (NC) courthouse, one night in 1830 Wright Allen crept up to and set fire to the courthouse burning it to the ground.

And then, during the Civil War, the Damn-Yankees burned the courthouse down again in 1862. These two arsons have created a 103 year gap, a black hole if you will, in the records for Hertford County, NC. which has and will forever plague genealogists and family history researchers.

As it turned out, the fraudulent note, IOU, bond was not in the courthouse the night it was burned in 1830. As for Wright Allen, he got his wish. He did not have to repay the money and he did not have to go to jail. **They hanged him.**

Last Will and Testament

At first it seems kind of humorous that the deceased might leave his silver spoons - one to each of his two daughters - or that one may instead get the pewter plate. A grandchild may get a cow and a calf when he/she comes of age. To each of the offspring, a shilling. To a child, the right size "wearing clothes" or, to a grandchild, the clothes "cut to fit". The copper pot was truly a treasure. Then comes the realization that the old wills seem humorous because we have become jaded from having so much. These meager items, that we today would take for granted, were all they had and they were given not with any notion that the children would be greatly enriched but that they were given a token of love and remembrance.

Occasionally, one of the old folks would deviate from the above. In the early 1800s, in one will a father left his son a plantation with the stipulation that to receive it he must not see a certain young widow any longer. He did not specify how he expected this provision of his will to be enforced or for how long. One would suppose that the younger brother who was to get the plantation in the event of a default, was keeping a sharp eye on the lover brother. Oh, what he would not have given for a camera with a telephoto lens.

Just as an aside, the term plantation in early Virginia was not what comes to the minds of most people, that being the huge fields filled with slaves picking cotton with the columned mansion in the background. In colonial Virginia, any plot or tract of land capable of having a crop planted was called a plantation. Tracts as small as thirty acres have been referred to as plantations.

William "Old Billy" Drake remembered all of his twelve children in his 1894 will, although not in way most would think. "To my sons John, William, George and Samuel, I leave nothing as they don't need it." Pragmatic to the end.

During the late 1700s and early 1800s, those making their wills developed the nasty habit of leaving the lands to one or two named offspring and the "movables to all my children". One can not help but think they did this just to thwart the latter day family researcher.

Also during this time frame, the soon to be deceased often would omit married daughters and children who had immigrated out of the area from their wills. Supposedly, married daughters now had husbands to supply their needs and those who had moved away were not going to return for a few inherited items.

It is not known why but draught animals never appear in wills. Where did all those oxen go? A favorite legacy was a cow, or better yet, a cow with a calf. These show up in wills very often. The earlier the will, the more likely someone gets a cow. But no one ever, ever is left a bull. Where did all those calves come from?

Never is anyone willed a chicken. No one is ever left a goose or a duck. Poultry gets a legacy pass. Could it have been some sort of fowl conspiracy? Or maybe the chickens did not survive the wake.

The Power of Prayer

For at least five generations, the Methodist Drake men of our part of the family have married Baptist women. Why is one of the great mysteries of the Universe. My very Baptist mother was one of seven siblings that lived to maturity, and all of them had children of their own. Twice a year, the second Sunday in July and the first Sunday after Christmas, this humongous family got together. At these gatherings, two things could be counted on: there was always a preacher invited, either Methodist or Baptist and occasionally both, and we children did not get to eat until after the adults.

The ministers always said grace before the meal. To hungry young'uns about to starve to death smelling the piles of food and knowing all the adults were to eat before we had a chance to dig in, having to suffer through a long, long, blessing was almost more than we could endure. We became experts in being able to tell the difference between a Methodist blessing and a Baptist blessing. And the difference is usually about a minute and ten seconds. Evidently Methodists get hungrier than Baptists.

Pot Luck

It seems that covered dish suppers are becoming a thing of the past. For those unfamiliar with the term, a covered dish supper is when some social group, be it church congregation, support group, or civic club, comes together for a meal with each member bringing some sort of dish for all to munch uponst (eat).

A theory has been developed that states the amount of fried chicken at a covered dish supper is directly proportional to the number of Baptists in attendance, whereas Methodists tend to favor ham and bar-b-que (the original plan was to say the Methodists **lean** toward ham and bar-b-que, which would have created an oxymoronic image as we Methodists are far too rotund to use the word lean).

As in the prior section, the observation regarding the blessing still applies - the Baptist blessing being a minute or so longer. Now, Methodist ministers are appointed to their charge by the Bishop so unless he, the Bishop, is in attendance, the minister has no need to display his oratory skills. Each Baptist minister, on the other hand, is hired by each individual congregation so each blessing or grace becomes an audition for his next job.

Wisdom of Granddaddy Rufus

"My feet are smelling and my nose is running,
I think I am put together up side down."

....And, as odd as it sounds, a still(noun) still(verb) does not stay still. It is still a movable.

Paternity Suit Proceedings

Against

Hugo Grant, Age 103

The following story is true, at least as I understand it. No names have been changed to protect the innocent; I do not think there are any innocents in this story. This story has to do with genes, but maybe not genealogy. It is a kind of history, but maybe not a family history. It is a story about family, but not my family as such. It is a story I thought would be better written down than lost to the dusts of time. There could be factual errors in this essay, but I do not think there are. If it turns out there are factual errors, then - oops! I'm sorry. If you found the previous section "Random Thoughts and Observations" interesting, you should like this – maybe – I hope.

Hugo Grant, you are my hero! How can a man who gets slapped with a paternity suit at the age of 103 not be a hero to all us aging males over 60? This story falls under the category of "you just can't make this stuff up".

Hugo was born August 10, 1910, to an unwed teen mother on the Thomas H. Drake farm. Hugo's grandfather, Richmond Grant, was a proud man who, upon learning his unwed daughter was pregnant, whipped her unmercifully. Granddaddy Rufus said you could hear her cries at the home place about 400 yards across the field. It has been speculated that Richmond Grant was born to slave parents about the time that the Confederate capitol of Richmond fell to the Union Army and General Grant - thus the name. Religious as well as proud, every Sunday he would pause to converse with Granddaddy Rufus on his walk through the woods and across the Great Cypress Swamp to ring the church bell at Mt. Gilead AME church for Sunday services.

As Hugo grew older, he worked on the farm with Granddaddy Rufus and his brother Uncle J.T. (James Thomas) until about 1931, at which time the great depression took its financial toll. Hugo, accompanied by his mother, decided that the city of Suffolk offered better opportunities in those trying times. Hugo did find a more lucrative line of work, moonshining. (Moonshining – manufacturing should not be confused with boot legging – distribution). His biggest problem at this time was with quality control - he tended to sample his product to excess.

One day (or it may have been night) after sampling his product a bit too much, Hugo found himself short of cash. He went to his mother for money. He got no money, but he did get enraged. Upon leaving the house cashless, he paused on the street, pulled a gun, and shot into the house. It is not known if Hugo intended to harm anyone in his drunken state or not, but the shot he fired hit and killed his mother.

The name of Hugo's mother is not known, but what is known of her seems a bit tragic. Pregnant as a teen by a man by the name of Stephenson, she was not able to force him to support little Hugo because he lived just across the state line in North Carolina and no Virginia laws could be brought to bear to force child support. Then Stephenson married someone else. Caught in the Great Depression, her only source of income seemed to be her son that she joined in Suffolk only to be shot and killed by him.

Hugo was charged with capital murder. His court-appointed attorney was trying his first case. A plea deal was struck. To avoid a death sentence, Hugo pled guilty and received a life without the possibility of parole sentence. So about 1933 Hugo was off to Spring Street in Richmond to the Virginia State Penitentiary where he spent the next 25 years of his life. (My Grandmother every year would collect the good peanuts from the ground that managed to escape the peanut picker. She would sew these up in small burlap bags (about 5 to 10 pounds) and then send them to friends and relatives across the country. Every year he was in prison, Hugo received a bag of peanuts at Christmas.)

To the prison officials, Hugo seemed to be a model inmate. His small loan-sharking business among the other inmates was never discovered, although the officials did wonder why, upon occasion, some member of another inmate's family would deposit money into Hugo's prison account. After a few short years, Hugo was made a trustee and given a job just outside the prison walls – custodian of the death house and the electric chair he had managed to avoid.

It has been said that with age comes wisdom. Maybe it does, maybe it does not. What does come with age is the realization of opportunities lost. I spent my late pre-teen years and my teen years listening to the tales of Hugo's prison life as we chopped (weeded, hoed) peanuts. If I knew then what I know now, I would have written them down: like the day the state executed six people in one day. As the custodian, Hugo had to be there. Or how you always eat your dessert first at meals in case there is a fight or riot in the dining hall and the resulting lockdown interrupts your meal half- eaten. Or how one day you happen to be looking out your cell window to see a bed sheet drop over the wall and several inmates slide down the sheet to casually walk away down Spring Street. Countless other tales are now forgotten and gone forever.

Usually Hugo's tales would end in "The Belly Laugh". A belly laugh for most people starts low in their chests; Hugo's seemed to start in the soles of his feet and bubble up and expand until it erupted out of his mouth and literally ended with his head thrown back looking at the sky and howling. It was the highlight of everyone's day to hear "The Belly Laugh". One sunny spring day sitting in the prison yard, Hugo was napping against the wall with his shirt off.

Guard on the wall: "Hey Grant, what-cha doing, getting a tan?"

Hugo: "Naw-sir Capt'n, just gettin' a shine." The Belly Laugh

Another day, guard in the tower: "Hey Grant, see that rat across the yard?"

Hugo: "Yessir I see him, he's a big'un."

BANG!!!! "Go get him and bring him back". Hugo retrieved the rodent.

Guard: "Shot him through the left eye, didn't I?"

Hugo: "yes sir, you sure did." Guard: "Remember that." NO laugh.

Like my Grandmother at Christmas, Hugo's court-appointed attorney had also not forgotten Hugo and his first case and wondered if he might not have done better. By that time, in 1958, Mills E. Godwin had attained a position of some prominence within the Democrat Party of Virginia. Having been sentenced to life without the possibility of parole, the only way for Hugo to be released from prison was a pardon from the Governor and this is what Godwin sought for his client. (Mills E. Godwin went on to be elected Governor of Virginia twice). The Governor agreed to a conditional pardon: if he had a job waiting for him on the outside, and agreed to supervision by a probation officer, Hugo would be released. The deal was endorsed by the prison warden.

Granddaddy Rufus:"We got a call from some lawyer fella in Suffolk by the name of Godwin. Says if we can give him a job, he can get Hugo released on parole."

R. E., Jr.: "I don't know about hiring a convict and a convicted murderer at that."

Granddaddy Rufus: "I think you should give him a try."

R. E., Jr.: "Daddy, when Hugo left the farm, we were using mules. Now we are using tractors and he has never driven one in his life. I don't think it will work."

Granddaddy Rufus: "I'll tell the lawyer we say yes."

So it came to pass in 1958 that Hugo Grant was released from prison on a conditional pardon to spend the next forty-plus years on the farm. Of the money he earned he spent nothing but what it took to live, and he lived Spartan. The only money I know him to have spent was for a stained-glass window in memory of Richmond Grant, his grandfather, at Mt. Gilead, AME.

It would seem that in 1930 Hugo fathered a daughter, Sue, who like her father was born out of wedlock. How much contact they had over the years he was incarcerated is not known, but they did have contact after he was released. It seemed to Hugo they got along well. So sometime in the late eighties, when Sue decided to build a house in Suffolk, she convinced her father to give her $10,000 of his savings to build a room in the new house for the purpose of him having a place to live when he retired or rather could no longer live on his own.

This was all well and good until Sue decided to sell the house at a good profit and did not give Hugo his investment back. That pretty much ended the father/daughter relationship. A bit later, when her mother died, Sue somehow managed to end up with her mother's house to the exclusion of her half-sister. Having signed his pay check for more than thirty years, when Hugo made his will, he made my mother his executor and warned her to watch out for Sue as he believed her to be a gold digger and scam artist and did not want her to have anything of his.

Around the year 2010, when he was approaching 100, Hugo finally had to admit he could no longer look after himself and went to a nursing home that took everything he had but $1,500 - and took his Social Security. And true to form, Sue began calling my mother wanting to know what kind of life insurance he had (he had none, but had prepaid his funeral years before), what was in his will (my mother did not know), or if he had any hidden accounts (to date, none have appeared). Hugo had said to watch her for he thought Sue was up to no good!

Then in 2013 Hugo was served with a paternity suit by Sue who wanted to prove that Hugo was her father by forcing him to have a DNA test. What she had in mind is unknown, but Hugo knew it was not good. And for the second time in his life, Hugo was appointed a lawyer by the court. A hearing was scheduled to determine if the court would compel a DNA test. His lawyer went to see Hugo in the nursing home.

Lawyer: "Mr. Grant, I have a subpoena here ordering you to appear in court on this matter with your daughter."

Hugo: "Ain't goin"

Lawyer: "But Mr. Grant, this is a subpoena from the judge. You have to go."

Hugo: "I am not going. What they going to do, put me in jail? Been there. Like it better than here. Nobody steals from you in jail. They going to fine me? Got no money. Ain't goin."

Hugo's lawyer reported back to the judge, who obviously did not know what to do. He could order the sheriff to go get him, but no one was fond of that idea. That would have looked really bad, physically forcing a

103 year old man in a wheel chair from a nursing home into court. What if he died in the process? The judge continued the case until the next month.

Next month, same thing. Hugo isn't going and no one dares to force him. Case continued. Third try, Hugo is still in his room and isn't going to come out. The judge finally has an idea: he tries the case with Hugo in absence, finds in Hugo's favor, and dismisses the action. Final score: ancient guy 3, legal system 0.

I know this is not what you expected of the paternity suit when you started reading but, get real, the man was 103 and in a wheel chair!

Hugo passed away two years later. Sue was notified. She did not come to the viewing or the funeral. In his will, of the money Medicaid allowed him to keep, Hugo left a bit to a kind young lady who cared for him as best she could, a bit to a young teen in his church, and he left $200 to be used to feed the people who came to the funeral. Hugo was laid to rest in the Mt. Gilead cemetery. Mt. Gilead AME church was over-full that day.

And the moral of the story is: No one should be above the law, but sometimes someone outlives it.

For those readers who are wondering what this chapter and the one that came before it are doing in a work of genealogy and probably think that it should not be here – you are absolutely right. The Author welcomes any and all complaints; it will show him that someone has read it.

REMEMBRANCES OF HUGO

A while back I wrote an essay about a paternity suit against Hugo Grant, age 103. I like to think of it as a "got-cha" piece in that it had probably an unexpected ending. But upon re-reading the essay I realized it conveys very little about Hugo the person. Most people who have passed have family and loved ones to keep their memories alive. For all practical purposes, Hugo has none. I hope to rectify that.

He stood about five ten – lean but muscular, ramrod straight. I remember thinking him to be the tallest person I had ever seen (a matter of perspective. When you are 4-5 years old and only three feet tall, all adults seem to be giants.) Hugo had only a minimum of formal education, but still, he was of above-average intelligence.

When he first came back to the farm in 1958, he lived in the house in which he was born across the road from where my father built his house in 1954. It had no bathroom, kitchen, or running water. No electricity. He carried water in buckets from our house across the road. He heated his water and cooked his breakfast and supper on a tin wood stove. Yet every morning when he came to work, he was clean and his work khakis were always cleaned and pressed. He washed his clothes by hand on the tin stove in a dish pan, hung them out to dry, and then pressed them with an old fashion iron heated on the stove. It was a rough existence to be sure, but one which was highly preferable to the cell in the Virginia State Prison where he had spent 25 years of his life.

While he was working, Hugo ate his lunches (we called it dinner) with us, our family – Daddy and Mama, my two older brothers and me, and, after June of 1959, our baby sister. With all of us there, the kitchen table was full, so Hugo ate at the kitchen counter. I believe the reason he stayed on the farm for 50 years, more or less, was Mama's cooking.

About 1962 or '63, Hugo bought the smallest house trailer ever. It had a combination living room/kitchen, a little bath, and a bedroom. But it did have an LP gas stove/oven and furnace. And it had a refrigerator. That was a giant improvement over the old house across the road

Three-quarters of a mile down Cypress Swamp Road from the old house where Hugo lived is the Railey Farm. It was owned by brothers Richard (Dick) and Russell Railey. Our father began working the farm on half-shares in 1947 or '48. There beside the road was a small clearing in the woods with a pair of large white oak trees to one side. The brothers offered Hugo a life-right to that spot to put his trailer under the shade of the oaks. Hugo accepted the offer but saw no need to have the area surveyed and a life-right filed at the courthouse – a waste of money and he tended to avoid courthouses as much as possible. And although he now had a bathroom, he saw no need to spend money on a well and septic system. He was quite happy with his little outhouse and "sinking a pump."

"Sinking a pump" – Ok city folks and young'uns, country education time. Southampton County, being in the Tidewater region of the east coast, averages about 45 feet above sea level. Because it is so low, the water table is close to the surface, as little as 2 feet in really wet times and low areas and generally never more than 10 to 12 feet below the surface. Often when the old folks needed water at a remote location, they would take a hand auger and bore a hole in the ground 2 to 3 inches in diameter to below the top of the water table, put in a pipe, affix a hand pitcher pump to the top of the pipe, and make some sort of small wooden structure to hold the pump and prevent ground water from seeping in the pipe hole. I think it impossible to hand pump the water from the hole faster than it would flow back in. And they called this process "sinking a pump."

Russell, the younger of the Railey Brothers, was the same age as Hugo. I like to think that their being the same age and born and raised only ¾ of mile apart maybe they played together as young'uns, but I have no idea that it might be so. I do know they knew each other well. As adults they took wildly divergent career paths: Russell went into law enforcement, Hugo went into the state penitentiary. At the time of Hugo's pardon/parole, Russell was the senior deputy sheriff in Southampton County.

Russell on more than one occasion made a comment that reflected Hugo's character. Russell said if he had to send a million dollars in cash to California, he would pick Hugo to carry it for him because he knew tha,t if Hugo made it, every penny of the money would make it too. What he did not know and wondered about is how many men Hugo would kill in the process to protect the money. In short, he thought Hugo extremely honest and very dangerous.

Sometime in the late 1960's early '70's, our little community got its second convicted killer returned from the Virginia State Penitentiary. Mark Luke Beale was paroled after serving 20 years for either manslaughter or second degree murder. All the other Blacks were scared of Mark Luke Beale - and Mark Luke Beale was scared of Hugo Grant. None of the other Blacks would even think about making Mr. Grant mad. Having been custodian of the death house for around 20 years, no other Black had seen as much death as Hugo and that fact seemed to make them very uneasy. They were never sure if he were carrying a gun or not and Hugo would have not said if he did or did not – let them wonder. Hugo did nothing to promote their fears of him, but he did nothing to alleviate their apprehension of him either.

As a convicted felon, it was illegal for Hugo to own a gun, but he did. How he got it is not known. When he left for the nursing home, he gave it to my father with instructions to give it to me at some point. Neither Hugo nor my father ever fired the gun, both boxes of ammunition were still full. It took an hour or more of maintenance and oiling to get it back in proper working condition. The Colt .32 long Police Positive Special is a cherished possession in my gun cabinet.

As for us boys, my two brothers and me, we had absolutely no fear of Hugo. It never occurred to us and he gave us no reason to think he might be dangerous. I can't say he was like a member of the family, but we felt he was much, much more than a hired hand. He always had, or made time, to talk with us and ask what was going on in our lives. When we were working weeding peanuts, Hugo kept us working and engaged by telling some of his stories. Ah-Hell, maybe he was a member of the family. But one thing was for certain: wherever he was, somehow his presence commanded respect (from everyone) and after nearly seventy years, I still can't explain it. My brothers on occasion will say Hugo worked for our father. He did not. Hugo worked **for** no one, but he worked **with** us for nearly 40 years.

At this point in this narrative, all the salient points of Hugo's character have been illustrated. The wise writer would realize the intelligent thing to do would be to stop writing.........I shall continue.

So, if you read the preceding companion piece to this essay, you know Hugo was sent to the Virginia State Prison, convicted of the murder of his mother for which he was sentenced to life without the possibility of parole. The only way for Hugo to be released was a pardon from the governor. Hugo's was a conditional pardon requiring parole supervision and a job. That job was provided by our father. Our father hired Hugo because he was more or less strong-armed into doing so by our grandfather.

So, if you read the preceding companion piece, you also know that our Grandmother for years would pick up peanuts left by the peanut picker to be sewn up in 5 to 10 pound burlap bags and sent to friends and family across the country. And that for 25 years Hugo always got one of those bags at or about Christmas. Daddy hired Hugo. Daddy was pressured by Granddaddy Rufus. I very strongly suspect that Hugo coming to the farm was what Grandmama Edna wanted. Grandmama never asked for much, but no one would ever deny her what little she wanted.

All this must be viewed through the lens of home and family. For the first twenty plus years of his life, Hugo grew up and worked on our family's farm. His grandfather, Richmond Grant, lived on the farm and worked with Granddaddy Rufus and Uncle J. T. as did Hugo from the time he was able work until he left with his mother for Suffolk. When he was paroled, Hugo came HOME – a home in which he would spend over 75 years in total of his very long life.

Now that your humble author is in his "golden" years, he has come to understand that, although Hugo legally owned none of the farm - which he knew, he looked upon the farm as his. Although Hugo was of no kin and of another race, he looked upon our family as his. He had nothing and no one else. That devotion was never betrayed by either Granddaddy Rufus, Grandmama Edna, or our father R. E., Jr.

Barnes Methodist Church was founded about 1794. During the first 70 years of its existence, slaves attended services either in the balcony or outside at a bush altar when one of their own was preaching. Some free Blacks, however, were members of the church as recorded by the Reverend Joshua Leigh in his journal of 1840 and beyond where he listed members of his churches. At the end of the Civil War, the former slaves and free Blacks established their own church – Mt. Gilead, AME (the land upon which they built was donated by a white member of Barnes.) They may have decided to build on their own or the members of Barnes may have suggested they would be happier elsewhere or maybe a bit of both. Whatever the case, I am aware of no Black attending any service at Barnes from 1865 to January of 1975 when, impeccably dressed, Hugo took a seat at the rear of the church for the funeral of Grandmama Edna. No one ever said a word of protest. This occurred again in February of 1978 for the funeral of Granddaddy Rufus.

Farming, especially row crop peanuts along with hogs and cows, can be a dirty business. You may start in the morning clean, but by night you are covered with dirt and dust. Or, if the day involved extended work with the livestock, even worse than dust and dirt. Hugo would get just as dirty as any of us, sometimes more so. But when he wasn't working with us or in his patch of peanuts or garden, Hugo was almost fastidious in his dress and grooming. He did not spend a whole lot of money on anything but, while not extensive, he did keep and maintain a small but impressive wardrobe.

In those days, late '50s and the '60s, farm workers did not make very much money. In those days, the farmers did not make very much money, especially if you had three or four children to feed and clothe. We did not have a lot of anything, us or Hugo. What we did have were gardens, livestock and peanuts. To supplement his income every year, when Daddy R.E. would decide how to rotate the crops, he always found a 5 acre field to plant in peanuts (in addition to those planted elsewhere in larger fields.) These were Hugo's peanuts. Daddy supplied the seed and fertilizer which would be reimbursed when the crop was harvested, and he supplied the equipment and fuel at no charge. Hugo supplied the labor. Many is the Saturday afternoon that Hugo was in his peanut patch pulling weeds and tending the plants.

And Hugo had gardens (plural). There was a small one in the clearing where his little house trailer stood and down the road, a half mile or so, he had a large one at the site of the old Railey homeplace. This one he worked on halves with Russell Railey (the deputy sheriff). None of us had much money or things, but we ate really well.

There was an old barn at the Railey house where Hugo had the big garden with Russell. Hugo stored his garden tools in the barn. As irate as I have ever seen Hugo is when someone made off with the garden hoe and prong fork that he kept in the old barn. I was standing with Daddy R.E. and Russell had just driven up in uniform in the county police car when Hugo discovered the thief. Hugo was talking to himself and shaking his head as he went to Daddy's truck to borrow a hoe. Russell watched all this. His only comment was "I pray he never finds out who took that hoe." Would Hugo have killed a man over a garden hoe? Russell was convinced he would.

Hugo kept those gardens until he was well into his nineties. Family members would encounter Hugo walking the half-mile between gardens: "Hugo, you want a ride to the garden?" "Nope, gotta walk to keep my bones loose." Of course he could not eat all he produced so most of it he gave away.

And then there was hog killing. Every year early in January when it was apt to stay cold, we killed hogs. We had lots and lots of hogs. Hogs contributed a large part of the farm's income. Generally, we would kill about 9 or 10 each year. Our family got 6 (a ham a month), Granddaddy and Grandmamma 2 or 3, and Hugo 1 or 2. This was a two-day affair. The first day, the hogs were killed, the hair on them scalded off, and the hogs gutted and hung up to cool in the January air. The livers were salvaged for supper that night, and the intestines were cleaned inside and out to make sausage casings and chitterlings. Thus ended day one.

On day two, the hogs were cut into hams, shoulders, middlings (side meat or bacon), pork chops and tenderloins. Daddy R. E. and Hugo would take the hams, shoulders, and middlings to the smokehouse to pack them in salt. The other parts of the hog were cut up either to make sausage or, if excessively fat, put into a big cast iron pot over a wood fire to render it into cracklings and lard. Cracklings are the lean meat part of the process once the fat had been melted away. They were scooped out of the pot, wrapped in an old bed sheet, and pressed between two wooden paddles to drain any remaining fat. The remaining fat was put into "lard stands" – 2 to 3 gallon reusable cans with removable tops – to cool and solidify into lard. Vegetable shorting it wasn't, but things cooked with it were really good, not very healthy but really good.

Most of the lard was used by Hugo. He cooked (fried) everything in lard sometimes twice a day. He used a lot of lard. Conventional wisdom says, eating that much pure animal fat, Hugo should have died an early death. He lived over 105 years. So much for the infallibility of modern health science.

I don't remember if Hugo got any sausage, but we made lots of it in two batches: one mild the way Daddy R. E., Jr. liked it, and one with lots of red pepper, the way Granddaddy Rufus liked it. It was frozen both in links and patties. The hog killing ended with a meal of sausage, fried tenderloin, crackling bread, and scrambled eggs with hog brains which the old folks loved and I have yet to this day had the courage to try. We did not have much money or things, but we ate really, really well.

After a bit Daddy and Hugo would "tear up" the meat and repack it in salt again. A bit later they would tear it up again, rub the meat with brown sugar and black pepper, and hang it in the smokehouse. Hugo usually did the smoking of the meat using a combination of hickory, apple, and oak sawdust. This is the way pork has been cured and preserved for more than 200 years in our area. Most people have heard of the famous "Smithfield Hams." Smithfield is part of our area. Those hams used to be cured as we cured ours. We always thought ours were a bit better. Today Smithfield uses a lot of modern production methods to shorten (and cheapen) the process, including an artificial hickory smoke. It isn't the same anymore.

The relationship between Hugo and Daddy R. E. is a bit hard to understand, and harder to explain. When Hugo left the farm for Suffolk and then prison, Daddy would have been only 5 or 6 years old. It is doubtful he remembered Hugo from the time before he left. Hugo, however, would certainly have remembered the little boy running around the farm he had watched grow from a baby, to a toddler, to a young boy. When Hugo returned, the young boy he knew was now a man of 31 approaching middle age and, having been off to war, was now raising a family of young sons, one of which, me, was of the same age my father had been when Hugo left. Although I am sure he had to, I do not recall ever hearing my father tell Hugo what he had to do. Hugo knew what had to be done that he could do and he did it. For his part Daddy R. E. would use Hugo for a sounding board, telling him what was going on with the farm and his hopes for the immediate future. Hugo would ask small questions and, only on rare occasions, offer his advice which was usually sound.

Hugo did this without ever complaining about the work – except once. Daddy rented a farm that was literally two miles back in the woods. The person who had previously worked the land used an old fashioned stationary peanut picker (as opposed to a combine). The old pickers would leave large piles of peanut vines wherever they had been set down and used at various places in the field. Hugo and I had to pack a lunch, take an old model "B" Farmall International tractor with an even older Massey Harris manure spreader, go to this field in the woods (complete with deer flies and mosquitoes), load the peanut vines in the spreader using pitch forks, and spread them over the field. This was a full day of very hard work.

Hugo: "I don't know what we did to be put out here but, if your Daddy will tell me, I'll promise never to do it again."

When my oldest brother went to basic training for the National Guard, about every other day Hugo would ask Daddy R. E. if he had heard from him and how was he doing. When my next oldest brother went off to college, about twice a week Hugo would ask if he had been heard from and how he was doing. I wasn't around to hear if he asked about me when I left for college, but he did ask about our sister when she went.

Hugo learned to use the tractor – some, but he did not like or care for tractor work. He would rather clean the hog droppings and disinfect the furrowing house (a hog delivery room and nursery). He learned to drive enough to move a truck from farm to farm but never obtained nor wanted a driver's license. Walking out in the open country suited him fine – understandable given he spent 25 years caged where he could do no walking. He would, however, accept a ride to Mt. Gilead AME every Sunday.

Our week ended on Saturday at noon, except during harvest time. Hugo would eat his lunch, reach into his shirt pocket and pull out his little notebook and pencil, and read his working hours to our mother…Monday 9 ¼, Tuesday 8, Wednesday 8 ½……Hugo kept up with his time on the job and he always had his little notebook and pencil with him. I don't know what he was paid, never asked. But it was more than us boys who worked for our room and board (well, not exactly, at the end of the year Daddy would put a bit in a savings account for each of us).

I think the last time Hugo had any liquor was the night he killed his mother. He made and drank a bit of homemade wine but, as for any other form of alcohol, I think he spent the last 75 to 80 years of his life as a teetotaler. He learned his lesson the hard way, but he did learn it.

Hugo was not a person to be led, nor was he a person who tended to follow the crowd. He did his own thinking, at times to the consternation of others. Generally he kept his thoughts to himself but, if one were to ask him his opinion, he gave it. It was somewhere around 1967-68 that Daddy R. E., Hugo and I were going from one farm to another on the pickup truck when Hugo relayed something which seemed to trouble him a bit for one reason or another. That weekend some Black clergy from the "City of Franklin" were making the rounds in the surrounding countryside, enlisting the aid of the locals. Something, I don't remember what, had happened in Franklin that had upset the Black residents – particularly the clergy. The conversation, as Hugo relayed it, went something like this:

Black Clergy: Brother Grant, I'm sure you heard of the trouble we have had in Franklin.

Hugo: I heard.

B. C.: Well, all the brothers and sisters are upset and we have decided to have a protest march.

Hugo: non-committal acknowledgement that he heard.

B.C.: We have decided to invite the Reverend Dr. Martin Luther King to come march with us. And he says he will come. All we need to do is send him (at this point I have forgotten the dollar amount, but for the mid-sixties it was huge - something on the order of $10,000 to $20,000) for his expenses. We are collecting the funds to get him here.

Now they had Hugo's full attention.

Hugo: Ah hell!!, he ain't coming here to help us, he's coming here to help his self! -----rapid exit of the Black Clergy.

Thus began, and ended, Hugo's foray into social activism.

Now that I have had the benefit of over 5 decades to think about it, I have come to the conclusion that Dr. King never had any intention of coming to such a low profile, backwater place like Southampton County, Virginia. At that time, he probably was getting 10 or more such requests from other backwater places each week. Rather than tell them no and seeming as if he did not care, he made his expenses so high that none of the requests would ever come to fruition.

Almost done, just a couple more remembrances. Whenever we would have a somewhat special supper, like a big fish fry or a big pot of chicken pie or for Christmas or for Easter, Mama would always fix a plate for Hugo. None of us got to eat until someone carried Hugo his plate. When there is food involved, you would be amazed at how fast someone can carry a plate a mile and a half down the road and get back.

We seldom knew what we were going to get for Christmas, but we all knew what Daddy was going to give Hugo for Christmas. The little burlap bag of peanuts was replaced by a whole carton of Apple Chewing Tobacco, a box of Prince Edward Cigars, and a check. Just now it occurred to me that the only presents my father ever bought in person for anybody were what he gave Hugo at Christmas.

When he was nearly 100 years old, Hugo went to a nursing home. For the five-plus years he was there, no week ever went by that my father did not go to see Hugo. Hugo hated the place. He said the employees were always taking what candy and goodies people would bring him. No Apple chewing tobacco, no Prince Edward cigars. He was getting deaf and the nursing home would not let him play his TV as loud as he would have liked. After a couple of years, they took away his cane – he threatened a few too many people with it. But his mind stayed sharp until the end. Being in the nursing home as he was, I am not sure his sharp mind was a good thing.

The last thing I did for Hugo was at the funeral home after he passed away. The funeral director came to me and said that, although Hugo had prepaid his funeral twenty or more years ago, the price of things specified were now higher than the price that Hugo had paid. I asked the funeral director how many funerals a year did he conduct – 30 to 35 or more. That was 600 to 700 funerals that he had the use of Hugo's money. Taking those 600 or 700 funerals multiplied by his profit margin, say 10, 20 percent or more, this gave him a giant return on Hugo's deposit. Hugo's money had made him probably twenty times the amount Hugo paid. If anything, he owed Hugo's estate a rebate. Hugo got the funeral for which he paid and a bit more.

Hugo's grave is next to the road across from Mt. Gilead, AME. The graveyard is adjacent to a farm Daddy R. E. bought in 1967. I go past his grave probably ten or more times a week. I always speak to him as I go by. "Old man, you are not forgotten."

This is an essay done for the Southampton Historical Society website circa 2006

Revision 6

The Founding and Founders Of Barnes Methodist Church, Southampton County, Virginia

By Joe H. Drake

Prologue

This is a revision of an earlier essay. The original was posted to the Southampton Historical Society's website in the "files" section. As a result of that posting, two gifted genealogical researchers, Margaret Van Ness Nelson and Peggy Vaughan McKinney, have located and contributed information that helps in the telling of the founding of Barnes Methodist Church. Their information has been incorporated into the text or footnotes.

The most significant of this information is a chancery case unearthed by Margaret: *Barnes vs. Edwards* September 18, 1798. The original premise of this essay was that Barnes Methodist Church was probably founded earlier than the generally accepted date of 1803. Within the materials contained in *Barnes vs. Edwards* is a sworn affidavit by one Samuel Woodard in which he recalls a conversation held at "Barnes Meeting House" in early 1794 (Southampton County, Virginia, Chancery Court Papers 1789–1801, Index Number 1798-0018, Library of Virginia, Richmond, Virginia). This now becomes the earliest written reference to Barnes Methodist Church.

Introduction

To date, the earliest written record of Barnes Methodist Church is the deed [1] (While still the earliest known record of the Church, it is not the earliest written reference to the church. See the Prologue above.) by which Jacob Barnes conveys the property to the trustees of the church: Benjamin Barrett, Benjamin Barnes, Exum Everett, Evans Pope and Nathan Britt/Brett[2]. The deed is dated January 22, 1803. Within that deed is a passage that prompted this essay (see appendix for full text of deed).

> "the said Jacob Barnes hath granted, bargained and sold and by these presents doth bargain and sell unto the said Benjamin Barrett, Benjamin Barnes, Exum Everett, Nathan Britt and Evans Pope their heirs and assigns forever one acre of land **with a meeting house thereon"** (emphasis added)

The implication of this is quite clear. At the time of the deed transferring the property to the trustees, the meeting house that would come to be known as Barnes Church had already been built on the property. Jacob Barnes was not transferring any one acre; he was transferring the acre with the meeting house (church).

---

[1] Southampton County Deed Book 10, page 119. Made January 22, 1803, recorded July 19, 1803.

[2] The surnames Britt and Brett are often confused. During the 1600's, 1700's and early 1800's, when less than half the population was literate, it was quite common for a clerk to spell a name phonetically. This led to many misspellings of names. Those who had their names misspelled, not being able to spell, never knew the difference. With the surname Britt or Brett it was very common to see the name of an individual spelled one way on one document and another on a later document, and occasionally to have his named spelled both ways on the same document. However it is believed, but yet to be absolutely proven, that all Britts and Bretts in southeastern Virginia and northeastern North Carolina are descendants of a John Britt who died in Isle of Wight County about 1695. The vast majority of Nathan Britt/Brett's known descendants spell their name Brett.

When was the original Barnes Church built? It was earlier than January 22, 1803, according to the deed. To perhaps answer this question, it is helpful to examine those involved – the grantees (the first trustees of Barnes Methodist Church), the grantor Jacob Barnes, and the father of Jacob Barnes also named Jacob.

Those Involved

This examination will begin with Jacob Barnes - but which Jacob Barnes. From a period beginning about 1700 to 1850, there were no fewer than nine men named Jacob Barnes in or near Southampton. They briefly are: (For the purpose of this paper, those involved with the deed conveying the land on which Barnes Church stands are in **bold**)

1. Jacob, a son of John Barnes of Isle of Wight, was born about 1707. This Jacob lived across the Nottoway River from where Barnes Church is located (St. Luke's Parish) in Nottoway Parish[3].
2. Jacob, a son of William Barnes, was born about 1730 and died 1810. Owned land in both Southampton County, Virginia and Wake County, North Carolina. His will gave no indications of any involvement with the church[4].
3. **Jacob,** a son of Edward Barnes, born 1735, died 1796. This was the father of both **Benjamin Barnes** and **Jacob Barnes** who were parties to the deed for the church[5]. Inherited the plantation from his father from which the acre for Barnes Church was taken. The area was known as Piney Woods in the 18th and early 19th centuries.
4. Jacob born 1750, died 1813, a son of yet another Benjamin Barnes. This Jacob lived and died in an area between present day Courtland and Capron. This area was called Buckhorn.[6]
5. **Jacob** born 1779, died 1856, son of **Jacob** (1735-1796) and brother of **Benjamin Barnes**. He was the grantor in the deed that transferred the property to the church.[7] [8]
6. Jacob born about 1805, son of Josiah. Josiah was a brother of **Benjamin** and **Jacob** of the deed (thus this Jacob was a nephew of these two men).[9]
7. Jacob born 1809, died 1865, was a son of Joshua. Joshua was also a brother to **Benjamin** and **Jacob** of the church deed.[10] (It is this Jacob who is ancestor to Carol Drake Majors.)
8. Jacob D., born about 1797, son of **Benjamin** Barnes of the deed and thus a nephew to **Jacob** of the deed. A Methodist Minister like his father, he removed to Iowa.[11]

---

[3] From the Genealogical Notes of Margaret Van Ness Nelson.

[4] Southampton County Will Book 7, will of Jacob Barnes of Southampton County Virginia and Wake County, North Carolina.

[5] Southampton County Will Book 4, page 723. Will of Jacob Barnes made September 15, 1790, recorded February 11, 1796. In it he names his children and wife.

[6] The Jacob from the Piney Woods area and the Jacob from the Buckhorn area were contemporaries and they both lived in the St. Luke's parish area of the county. If one looks at the land tax book for this period, they will see two Jacob Barnes listed. One will have PW (Piney Woods) behind his name; the other Jacob will have BH (Buckhorn) behind his.

[7] Southampton County Will Book 4, page 723. Will of Jacob Barnes (the elder) made September 15, 1790, recorded February 11, 1796. In it he names his children and wife.

[8] Southampton County Death Register Abstract page 26. James M. Barnes, executor of the estate and nephew, gives Jacob's date of death as March 13, 1857, and Jacob's age as 7. Thus Jacob was born in 1779.

[9] Southampton County Court Records, Chancery Order Book 1859-1882, page 145. Barnes vs. Barnes names Jacob as a son of Josiah.

[10] Southampton County Will Book 15, page 667. Will of Jacob Barnes made December 15, 1856, recorded March 16, 1857. Names Jacob as a son of his brother Joshua.

[11] Ibid, names Jacob D. as a son of his brother Benjamin.

9. Jacob, born 1843, was a son of Samuel. Samuel was another son of Josiah, brother to **Benjamin** and **Jacob** of the deed.[12]

Jacob Barnes (1735-1796)

Jacob Barnes (1735-1796), hereafter described as Old Jacob, owned more than 331 acres[13] located approximately where Darden Mill Run (the Cypress Swamp) crosses Sands Road and continues south past Barnes Church on Statesville Road and then east along Barnes Church Circle for about a mile. Old Jacob also owned more than 600 acres in Pitt County and 543 acres in Northampton County, North Carolina. He also owned 156 acres in Edgecombe County, North Carolina.

Old Jacob had ten children (7 boys and 3 girls):[14]

1. Benjamin, the eldest, born about 1761
2. Josiah, born about 1765
3. Thomas, born about 1769
4. Joshua, born about 1771
5. William, born about 1774
6. James, born about 1776
7. Jacob, born 1779 (hereafter **Young Jacob**, the youngest son).
8. Sela, born about 1763
9. Sarah, born 1767
10. Nancy Ann, born about 1777

At the execution of his will in 1790, Old Jacob left eldest son Benjamin land from about where Darden Mill Run crosses Sands Road west on Sands Road for approximately one-half mile.

Young Jacob was devised the land commencing where the land devised to Benjamin ended to where the church is today on Statesville Road. Today this land is owned in part by Claude Drake (a 5xG Grandson of old Jacob) and in part by Nancy Parker Matthews.

The home plantation was willed as a reversionary interest after the death of Old Jacob's wife to sons Thomas and Josiah. This is roughly the same land as the farms owned today by Boone Drake (a 5xG Grandson of old Jacob), and Carol Drake Majors (a 5xG Granddaughter of old Jacob).

To his sons Joshua and William, Old Jacob devised the land in Pitt County and to his son, James, he devised the land in Edgecombe County.

Old Jacob purchased the Northampton County, North Carolina, land after he made his will in 1790. After the death of his wife, Elizabeth, in 1802, it was sold between his children.

Jacob Barnes (1779 –1857)

Jacob Barnes (1779 – 1857) --"Young Jacob" herein -- was grantor of the deed to the church property. He was the youngest son of Old Jacob and most likely the youngest of all his children. In his will of 1856, he refers to

[12] Northampton County, North Carolina, Deed Book 38, page 100. Report of the commissioners to divide the estate of Samuel Barnes.

[13] Southampton County Land Tax Books, 1782 – 1796.

[14] Southampton County Will Book 4, page 723. Will of Jacob Barnes made September 15, 1790, recorded February 11, 1796. In it he names his children and wife.

the "one acre I deeded to the church" in describing the boundaries of the land he would devise to his nephew and executor of his estate James M. Barnes (son of Young Jacob's brother Joshua).[15]

Young Jacob was only age 17 when his father died in 1796[16]. It may be for this reason that the estate of Old Jacob seems not to have been closed until 1802.[17] No record of a guardian to protect the interest of the minor, Young Jacob, in regards to the will of his father has been found to date. This suggests that the estate of Old Jacob could not be closed until Young Jacob came of age. Rather than be troubled with a court-appointed guardian, Young Jacob's mother, Elizabeth, and his brother, Josiah, the executors of Old Jacob's estate,[18] may have postponed settling the estate until Jacob was of age 21.

On November 19, 1804, Young Jacob married Lucy Barrett, daughter of Benjamin Barrett, a trustee of the church.[19] Benjamin Barnes performed the wedding. In no census do Young Jacob and Lucy ever have any children within their household.[20] In his will of 1856, Young Jacob names several of his nieces and nephews, but makes no mention of any offspring.[21] So, Young Jacob and Lucy had no children, at least any who survived to maturity.

Benjamin Barnes (c. 1761 – c. 1828)

Benjamin Barnes, eldest son of Old Jacob, was an ordained Methodist Minister. Benjamin was admitted on trial to the Methodist Conference in 1788. In 1789 he was appointed to the Orange Circuit. In 1790 Benjamin was admitted to the Church with "full connections" and appointed a deacon of the Church; in other words, Benjamin had now become a fully ordained minister and Elder of the Methodist Church (Virginia Conference). He was appointed to the Bedford Circuit in that year. He was appointed to the Sussex Circuit in 1791, to the Brunswick Circuit in 1792, and to the Bertie, North Carolina Circuit in 1793.[22]

In 1793 or 1794 Benjamin left the traveling Methodist Circuit to come back to Southampton to raise his family. Benjamin was married to Linna Lee on January 22, 1795, in Gates County North Carolina.[23] It is not known at this time if Gates were a part of the Bertie Circuit to which Benjamin was assigned in 1793. If it were, it could well be that Benjamin met his wife-to-be while ministering to that Circuit. Within Benjamin's household in 1810 were 8 children: 3 males under 10 years of age, 2 males aged 10 to 16, a female under 10, a female between 10 and 16, and a female 16 to 26.[24]

---

[15] Southampton County Will Book 15, page 667. Will of Jacob Barnes made December 15, 1856, recorded March 16, 1857.

[16] Southampton County Death Register Abstract page 26. James M. Barnes, executor of the estate and nephew, gives Jacob's date of death as March 13, 1857, and Jacob's age as 77; thus Jacob was born 1779.

[17] Southampton County Land Tax Books, 1796 – 1803.

[18] Southampton County Will Book 4, page 723. Will of Jacob Barnes made September 15, 1790, recorded February 11, 1796. In it he names his children and wife.

[19] Southampton County Marriage Register, page 162. The marriage is also listed in the minister's returns by Benjamin Barnes.

[20] United States Census for Southampton County Virginia, for 1810 page 0058B, for 1820 page 0111A, for 1830 page 0249A, for 1840 page 0090A and for 1850 page 0268A.

[21] Southampton County Will Book 15, page 667. Will of Jacob Barnes made December 15, 1856, recorded March 16, 1857.

[22] The Minutes of the Conferences –1773-1813. Vol. 1. New York: Published by Daniel Hitt and Thomas Ware. (From Methodist Archives, McGraw Library, Randolph-Macon College, Ashland, Virginia). Provided by Margaret Van Ness Nelson.

[23] Via email to the author. From the Genealogical Notes of Peggy Vaughan McKinney

[24] United States Census for Southampton County, Virginia, for 1810, page 0055A.

An additional 2 males and 2 females under 10 years of age are shown in the household in the 1820 census. To date we have not learned which, but these additions to the household may have been children or even grandchildren.[25]

Linna is listed as the head of household in the 1830 census[26] probably revealing that Benjamin has died. In 1826 Benjamin was the grantee in a deed of trust executed to secure a debt owed to him,[27] thus Benjamin died between 1826 and 1830.

Oddly, Benjamin was perhaps the best educated of the first trustees of Barnes Church - probably better educated than his father or brother Jacob. Yet, Benjamin was the only one of the first trustees of Barnes Church who died intestate. Whether or not that fact reveals a sudden and unexpected death is not known.

Benjamin and Linna had either 8 or 9 children who survived to maturity. We are able to identify 8 of these thanks to Peggy Vaughan McKinney whose research revealed a chancery case to divide Benjamin's estate.

1. John E. Barnes[28]
2. Jacob Davis Barnes[29]
3. Robert S. Barnes[30]
4. Richard Barnes
5. Benjamin H. Barnes
6. Martha F. Barnes
7. Marmaduke N. Barnes
8. Mary Barnes
9. Nancy G. Barnes[31]

---

[25] United States Census for Southampton County, Virginia, for 1820, page 0111A. The 1850 census was the first to list all the people by name. Until that census, only the head of household was listed by name and the others in the household were listed by age only.

[26] United States Census for Southampton County, Virginia, for 1830, page 0248A.

[27] Southampton County, Virginia Deed Book 23, page 144. Benjamin names his brothers Thomas and Jacob as the trustees to the deed.

[28] Southampton County Will Book 15, page 667. Will of Jacob Barnes made December 15, 1856, recorded March 16, 1857. Names John E. as a son of his brother Benjamin living in Iowa.

[29] Ibid, Names Jacob D. as a son of his brother Benjamin living in Iowa.

[30] While no record has been found that directly says that Robert S. and Nancy G. Barnes were children of Benjamin Barnes, there is a convincing body of evidence that this is the case. (Note: direct records indicating that Robert was a son of Benjamin are now known to exist.} Nancy G. married Archer Vick and during the Civil War their home was the farm on which R. E. Drake, Jr. lives today. R. E. Drake, Jr. is a trustee of Barnes Church today, and is a 4xG Grandson of Old Jacob. Also among the trustees today are Willie Thomas Drake, a 4xG Grandson of Old Jacob who lives on the land left to Benjamin Barnes by Old Jacob, Roy E. Drake, a 5xG Grandson of Old Jacob, and Joe L. Everett, a 2xG Grandson of Exum Everett. Sadly, as of this revision (#6), Aug. 8, 2017, Willie Thomas Drake, Roy E. Drake, and Joe Everett have all passed away.

[31] Ibid

Nancy G. Barnes may or may not be a child of Benjamin Barnes. The writings dealing with the court case are faded and difficult to read. While there seems to be a child whose name begins in "N" in the caption for the case, the rest of the name can not be deciphered, and there is not mention of Nancy that can be made out in the following text of the case; however, most of the children of Benjamin Barnes were also not mentioned the text of the case.

Like their father, Jacob D. and Robert S. Barnes also became Methodist Ministers. Jacob removed to Iowa,[32] while Robert served more than 18 years as an assistant pastor to Barnes Church.[33] In addition, Robert was also a trustee to Mount Horeb church.[34]

Benjamin Barrett (c. 1750 – before 1813)

Benjamin Barrett, another of the first trustees of Barnes Methodist Church, was the son of Edmond Barrett and his second wife Jennet. There is some dispute among researchers as to who Jennet might have been. It seems there are two choices 1) Jennet Everett – a daughter of Simon Everett, who was grandfather of Exum Everett, one of the trustees named in the Barnes Church deed. Or 2) Jennet – the widow of Drury Bynum.[35]

One of Benjamin Barrett's daughters, Lucy, was to marry Young Jacob Barnes in 1804.[36] Jacob was the grantor of the deed to the Church.

Benjamin was married to Catherine Barnes. Catherine was the widow of Burwell Barnes, who died in 1777.[37] Burwell Barnes was a younger brother of Old Jacob. Catherine's parents were Joseph and Olive Taylor Simmons.[38]

Benjamin and Catherine were married January 20, 1785.[39] Benjamin and Catherine had seven children:[40] three boys and four girls. These were named in Benjamin's will. [41]

The children of Benjamin Barrett and Catherine Barnes were:

1. James Barrett

2. Jane Barrett

---

[32] Southampton County Will Book 15, page 667. Will of Jacob Barnes. Names Jacob D. as a son of his brother Benjamin living in Iowa

[33] Historical Record Barnes United Methodist Church, by Betty W. Darden, page 7.

[34] From the Genealogical Notes of Margaret Van Ness Nelson.

[35] Drury Bynum patented land circa 1740 that was the land or close to the land that R. E. Drake and Joe Everett live upon today.

[36] Southampton County Marriage Register, page 162. The marriage is also listed in the minister's returns by Benjamin Barnes.

[37] Southampton County Will Book 3, page 386

[38] Faye Thorpe Coats, Genealogical notes.

[39] Southampton County Marriage Bond Register, page 635.

[40] Catherine also had a son by her marriage to Burwell Barnes, Simmons Barnes.

[41] Southampton County Will Book 7, page 312. The will of Benjamin Barrett, made July 4, 1812, recorded November 1813. Names wife and children.

3. Lucy Barrett

4. Giles Barrett

5. Lydia Barrett

6. Ann Barrett

7. John Barrett

Benjamin's will was executed on July 4, 1812, and recorded in November of 1813.

As a matter of interest, Benjamin Barrett had a brother Burwell. Burwell was also a Methodist Minister.

Exum Everett (before 1765 – 1830)

Exum Everett was a son of Thomas Everett, Sr. and Elizabeth Edwards. Exum was also a Methodist Minister. In the minister's returns for Southampton County, located in the Southampton County Marriage Bond Register, there appear more than 75 weddings performed by Exum Everett.

Exum's wife was Elizabeth, maiden name unknown at this time. Exum and Elizabeth were to have nine children. These are named in Exum's will executed on February 9, 1830, and placed of record on March 3, 1830:[42]

1. Caleb

2. Thomas (Jr.)[43]

3. Henry

4. John

5. Samuel

6. Mason

7. Burwell (or Burrell)

8. Charlotte

9. Sidney

Sidney, the youngest daughter[44] of Exum Everett was to marry Jesse Brett on August 12, 1804.[45] Jesse was a son of Nathan Britt/Brett,[46] another of the first trustees of Barnes Methodist Church.

---

[42] Southampton County Will Book 10, page 230. The will of Exum Everett made February 9, 1830, recorded March 15, 1830.

[43] Special Note on the use of the terms junior and senior. In the records at the time before the Civil War, when few people had or used middle names, the use of the terms Junior and Senior did not necessarily represent a father and son, but rather a way to denote between two men within the records with the same name. These men may or may not have been related.

Nathan Britt/Brett (c.1757 –1815)

Of the first five trustees of Barnes Church, less is known of Nathan Britt than the others. We now have learned through a study of land deeds from which they were involved that the name of Nathan's father was also Nathan[47] and he - the older Nathan - was married to Charity[48] Gatling[49]. The first name of the wife of the younger Nathan (he of the Church deed) is known, Elizabeth, but her maiden name remains undiscovered. Judging from the census of 1810, Nathan lived beside Exum Everett; Exum being the last name on page 0059A and Nathan being the first name on the page following, 0059B.[50]

Nathan Britt's son, Jesse Brett, married Exum Everett's daughter, Sidney.[51] Exum was another of the first trustees of the church.

Nathan made his will in 1811 and added a final codicil to his will on February 19, 1815.[52] The will was placed of record on March 20, 1815. In it he named his children, and gave the first name of his wife. The children were:

1. John
2. Jesse
3. Nathan
4. Emmy
5. Elizabeth
6. William
7. Rhoda
8. Cherry

Evans Pope (c. 1760 – 1828)

The parents of (Benjamin)[53] Evans Pope have not yet been found. On January 30, 1787, Evans married Sarah Barnes[54] through the consent of her parents, Jacob and Elizabeth Barnes. Thus Old Jacob was Evans's

---

44 The order in which the children of Exum are listed is the order in which they are listed in the will. This is generally an indication of the birth order as well.

45 Southampton Marriage Bond Register, page 161. Sidney's name is misspelled "Cidney". Jesse's name is spelled "Britt" in the bond and "Brett" in the ministers returns.

46 See footnote 2, page 1.

47 The name Nathan Brett first shows up as a witness to a deed in what was then Bertie County, N.C. (Deed Book F, page 69) on 1 Jan. 1739. Therefore, this Nathan could be born no later than 1718-20. The area of Bertie in which this Nathan owned land would later become Northampton and then Hertford County. This older Nathan would have deeds in both as well as Southampton County, Virginia. The Southampton County tax list of the years 1782 to 1789 list both a Jr. and Sr. Nathan Brett as does Southampton Deeds Bk 5, page 237; Bk. 5, page 446; Bk.5, page 434.

48 Southampton County Deed Book 7, page 222. 11 June 1789. Nathan Brett and wife Charity to Edward Brett, 30 acres, "the last of my lands in Southampton"

49 Northampton County, North Carolina, wills 1757 - 1808. Will of Sarah Gatling (unmarried) names sister Charity Brett.

50 United States Census for Southampton County Virginia, for 1810, pages 0059A and 0059B.

51 Southampton Marriage Bond Register, page 161.

52 Southampton County Will Book 7, page 436. The will of Nathan Britt, made 1811, a codicil was added on February 19, 1815, and the will was recorded on March 20, 1815.

father-in-law. As the consent of her parents was required, Sarah was under the age of 21 at the time of her marriage.

Evans Pope executed his will on February 22, 1828.[55] The will was ordered to be recorded on March 17, 1828. In it he named his children.

1. Joseph Pope
2. Sally Pope
3. Elizabeth Pope

The Founding of Barnes Methodist Church
A *Probable* Scenario

In 1790 Old Jacob Barnes made out his will. His eldest son Benjamin was in Bedford County on the Methodist Circuit, so Old Jacob named his next eldest son, Josiah, executor, and named his wife Elizabeth co-executor.

In 1793 Benjamin Barnes left the Methodist Circuit and would marry a bit more than a year later.

In 1793, Benjamin Barnes and Exum Everett were ministers with a church (the congregation), but without a church building. Looking about the neighborhood, they found an ideal site for a meetinghouse. The point selected was where the Fish Road[56] (now Statesville Road), the Boone Road[57] (now Rochelle's Swamp Road) and the Cypress Road (now Sands Road) converge. The land was owned by Benjamin's father, Old Jacob Barnes.

Old Jacob committed to giving the land and construction began, but Old Jacob passed away before he could change the will or convey the land to the Church. (This paragraph is a bit speculative but based on known facts.)

The land upon which the Church was built was devised to Young Jacob. Under the law of the period, the title to the land could not vest in Young Jacob until he reached his 21st birthday. Thus it did not matter what anybody intended or hoped. Until that date the property could not be viewed as belonging to the Church, though it is suspected that the congregation occupied and used it as a church meetinghouse.

In late 1800 or early in 1801, Young Jacob reached the age of 21. The following year Young Jacob's brother and executor of their father's estate, Josiah, settled the estate. The year after, on January 22, 1803, Young Jacob conveyed the property by the deed discussed to the trustees of Barnes Methodist Church.

---

[53] Cemetery records compiled by Mrs. Bruce Phillips Saunders indicate a first name of "Benjamin" and a middle name "Evans". All the records of Southampton County and the will show the name "Evans Pope". Later, Evans' son Joseph would name his eldest son Benjamin Evans Pope.

[54] Southampton Marriage Bond Register, page 104

[55] Southampton County Will Book 10, page 85. The will of Evans Pope, made February 22, 1828, recorded March 17, 1828.

[56] As a matter of interest, if one were to follow the Fish Road south to its end, they would find that the road ended at the Meherrin River in North Carolina just east of Murfreesboro. At this point there was a seining beach where herring were caught by net during the spring, thus the name Fish Road.

[57] The Boone Road was named so because it ran to Boone's Bridge in the edge of N.C. crossing the Meherrin River.

Note that the deed that conveys the property to the church does not appoint Benjamin Barrett, Benjamin Barnes, Exum Everett, Nathan Britt and Evans Pope as the trustees to the church. In the latter part of the deed, after the bounds of the property were given, it was implied that these men had been nominated or elected as the trustees previously, thus their participation in the deed.[58] Such a nomination or election prior to the making of the deed would most likely have been by the members of the congregation of the church. This indicates an active congregation before the January 22, 1803, date of the deed. Young Jacob would have had no authority to appoint the trustees for the church and the wording of the deed seems to verify this.

The deed concludes by establishing the governance for the trustees of the Church. It is believed these guidelines reflected Methodist Doctrine of the era. A clause was also added to the deed that required those who would preach there to be Methodist Ministers. It is doubtful that Young Jacob, having just attained the age of 23, would have had the presence or maturity of mind to include such a statement in a deed. It is, however, exactly the type of wording an ordained Methodist Minister, Deacon, and Elder of the Church - of age 42 - would include in a deed. Benjamin Barnes was the likely driving force behind the deed to Barnes Methodist Church.

Among the first five trustees of the new church were Old Jacob's son (Benjamin Barnes), Old Jacob's son-in-law (Evans Pope), and the son of Old Jacob's brother-in-law (Benjamin Barrett). Exum Everett and Nathan Britt may have also had family connections with Old Jacob that are not now apparent.

Church lore has it that the Church was named for Jacob Barnes who donated the land. Research shows this is likely true. What has been lost through the last two centuries is the proof that the Jacob who gave the land, and the Jacob who conveyed the land by deed, were not necessarily the same Jacob, but rather father and son.

In his will of 1856, Young Jacob did not refer to the land of the Church as "the one acre I gave to the Church" nor "the one acre I sold to the Church", but rather "the one acre I deeded to the Church". The semantics of this statement have significance. Such a statement in a will worded in such a way is very rare but, if it was Old Jacob who had given the land for the church and Young Jacob fulfilling his father's intentions (by "deeding" the land), how else could he have described the land upon which the Church stands?

Human nature being what it is, it is hard to imagine Old Jacob's son, son-in-law, and son of his brother-in-law naming the Church after the baby brother of the family nearly 20 years or more their junior. It is very easy, however, to accept the likelihood that they would name the church for a recently departed father figure – Old Jacob Barnes.

Special note on the term "meetinghouse"

Prior to the Revolutionary War there was only one church, that being the Church of England which was supported by the state through taxes. Today this is the Episcopal Church. For any other group, be it Methodists, Baptists, Quakers, or any other, to use the term "Church" would have been illegal and treasonous. For this reason, the non-state supported sects adapted the term "meetinghouse" for their church buildings. Although the Treaty of Paris ended the revolution in 1783, the use of the term "meetinghouse" continued for some years after.

Appendix I

The text of the deed to the Barnes Church Property. DB 10: 119

[58] Based on an observation by Paul Drake, JD.

Deed for the lot of land on which Barnes now stands.

This Indenture made this 22nd day of January in the year of our Lord one thousand eight hundred and three, between Jacob Barnes of Southampton County and State of Virginia on the one part, and Benjamin Barrett, Benjamin Barnes, Exum Everett, Nathan Britt and Evans Pope, of the same County and State, aforesaid on the other part.

Witnesseth that in consideration of one dollar by said Benjamin Barrett, Benjamin Barnes, Exum Everett, Nathan Britt, and Evans Pope to the said Jacob Barnes truly paid before sealing & delivery hereof the receipt whereof the said Jacob Barnes doth hereby acknowledge and for diverse other consideration (to) him thereunto moving the said Jacob Barnes hath granted, bargained and sold and by these presents doth bargain and sell unto the said Benjamin Barrett, Benjamin Barnes, Exum Everett, Nathan Britt and Evans Pope, their heirs and assigns forever one acre of land with a meetinghouse thereon situated in the County and State aforesaid and bounded as follows,

Beginning at a pine tree being a corner tree between Jacob Barnes and Benjamin Barrett, thence a straight line 70 yards to a lightwood post, thence North by West 70 yards to a lightwood post, thence south by west 70 yards to a lightwood post, thence to the beginning. Together with all the ways and privileges to the said premises appurtaining thereunto, and all the profits thereof with all the right, titledge and interest in law and equity. To have and to hold the said land and other premises to the said Benjamin Barrett, Benjamin Barnes, Exum Everett, Nathan Britt and Evans Pope, their heirs and assigns forever. Nevertheless upon special trust and confidence and to the interest that they and the survivors of them and the Trustees for the time being do and shall permit the preachers of the Methodist Episcopal Church and no other persons to have and enjoy the free use and benefit of the said premises that they may therein preach and expound God's Holy Word from time to time and at all times forever; and upon further trust and confidence that as often as any of these trustees shall die, remove, or cease to be members of the Methodist Society, the Trustees for the time being as soon as conveniently may be, shall and may choose another Trustee or Trustees in order to keep up the number of five Trustees forever.

IN WITNESS whereof, the said Jacob Barnes hath hereunto set his hand and seal the day and year above written.

Signed: Jacob Barnes

Teste: Reuben Whitfield, Pilgrim Vick, Lucy Barrett, Betsey Whitehead

And the Spirit Moved Him

Earlier in the chapter entitled "Random Thoughts and Observations" I stated that I would tell the last of the brandy tales. I did. This story is about moonshine, not brandy. The last chapter on the founding of Barnes Methodist Church was an exercise in pure genealogical writing and local history. Unless one is interest in Barnes Methodist Church or one of the founding families, they probably found it somewhat dull and boring. I am a lifelong member of Barnes Methodist Church and two of the founding families are of direct descent. I wrote the darn thing and I find it somewhat dull and boring. It's time for a more fun tale.

Most of this tale was relayed by Granddaddy Rufus, he who thought his nose was running and his feet were smelling and he was put together upside down. Where he obtained the information, no one knows. Granddaddy Rufus would have been 26 when the main subject of this tale passed away one farm over from his.

The Reverend Davis Bryant was a God-fearing man of the cloth. The spirit moved him to preach the gospel - at least preach it when he wasn't busy trying to acquire more land. Davis served as the minister of Barnes Methodist Church for the years 1848 and 1849. He probably served as a "local" preacher to Barnes before that although the Church records do not reflect such. Rev. Davis Bryant loved the Lord. Evidently he also loved his wife, the former Lydia Barrett, with whom he had 13 children that survived to maturity.

In October, 1843, Davis Bryant and his brother Orman took the estate inventory of their father William Bryant, Jr. This is significant because it means William died intestate – without a will. That's not an exactly accurate statement so let me clarify: William had an inventory in the Will Books but no last will was found. This means that what land William Bryant, Jr. owned was divided as provided by law. His widow received 1/3 of the land – the dower share - and the remaining 2/3 would have been divided between his (gulp) twelve children.

So the Rev. Davis Bryant inherited little or no land. Yet at his death in his will he left each of his thirteen children a farm. It would seem that, when not preaching the word of the Lord, Davis was very much into making money and buying farms – in a Christian-like manner, I'm sure. The home place he left to his tenth child, a boy christened Richard Lewis Bryant who was born June, 1830. No one today knows why but, for some reason, Richard was called Toolly (pronounced Tool'-Lee). And that brings us to the main subject of this work, that being Toolly. With a name like Toolly there has to be some good tales.

Toolly was a part-time farmer and a full-time moonshiner. But prior to that, Toolly had served with the 9th Virginia Infantry during the Civil War. It is not known how much action or fighting Toolly had seen, but the 9th Virginia had seen a heaping big bunch. The regiment was at Seven Pines and the Seven Days in 1862. They were part of Armistead's brigade of Pickett's division during the charge at Gettysburg and were among the soldiers that reached the stone wall in the Union line - the "high tide" of the Confederacy. They were at Cold Harbor and in the trenches of Petersburg. When the 9th Virginia Infantry surrendered at Appomattox, there were two officers and thirty-six enlisted men left to parole. A Civil War regiment usually started out with a thousand men.

Toolly's father, the Rev. Davis Bryant, died in 1849, and his mother, Lydia Barrett Bryant, in 1862. So Toolly had no paternal impediments to starting his career upon his return from the war. He raised corn among other things but, unlike most other farmers, Toolly sold his corn crop not by the bushel, but by the gallon. Toolly died in 1915, five years before prohibition. It was hard to understand what the attraction of moonshining might have been. Some research was done on the matter. A brief history of alcohol taxation follows:

Moonshining got its start in western Pennsylvania when whiskey-making farmers there refused to pay a newly enacted excise tax on alcohol enacted by the Congress in George Washington's time as President. The irate Pennsylvanians even went so far as to tar and feather some of the revenue agents (hereafter known as revenuers). This became known as the Whiskey Rebellion. It ended when George Washington led a group of militia to belligerent areas. He collected the tax and then pardoned all involved. Peace was restored and all was well, except for a few who hid their stills and continued to make tax free whiskey – the first moonshiners. This tax was repealed after Thomas Jefferson became president.

With the advent of the Civil War, the Union was seeking ways to finance the war so an excise tax on alcohol was enacted once more. In time the Civil War ended; the excise tax on alcohol did not. Now this is important: one might wonder why the revenuers would go to so much trouble as to track down moonshiners at this time. Was it worth the effort for the government from an income standpoint? The answer is yes indeed. The tax was two dollars per alcohol gallon. An alcohol gallon is a gallon which is fifty percent (50%) alcohol. Most moonshine is at least 50% alcohol, and some nearly pure gain alcohol. Therefore, one can figure the tax on a gallon of moonshine at about three dollars. A run of 50 gallons of mash would produce about 5 gallons of moonshine depriving the poor federal government of about $15 dollars. Doesn't sound like a great deal of money by today's standards but in 1880 the average annual income per household was only $385 or a bit less than $26 per week. In tax money, a moonshiner could save as much in taxes in two days as the average worker could make in a week. The price advantage the moonshiner had over the taxpaying producer was huge.

Toolly used to hide his still in the Great Cypress Swamp which adjoined his farm to the east. And it is said that he sometimes set his still up on Possum Branch to the west of his property. I don't exactly know when but there was a time, according to Granddaddy Rufus, when you couldn't go a quarter mile along the Great Cypress Swamp without seeing a still busted up by revenuers. It is reasonable to surmise some of which would have been Toolly's. The Great Cypress Swamp in those days was about ten miles long and an average of a mile wide.

Sometime in the late 1860's after the war, Toolly married Margaret Lucretia Hill. Everyone called her Lou. By all accounts, Lou was a good, God-fearing woman who, according to Granddaddy Rufus, attended Barnes Methodist Church every Sunday. And Granddaddy Rufus would know as he was at Barnes every Sunday. Lou tried to raise their four children to be good Christian people and tried to help Toolly see the errors of his ways. It is not known if Lou was raised a Baptist (who are all supposedly decidedly anti-alcohol, at least in theory) but it is known she was very much against alcoholic beverages.

As Granddaddy Rufus told it:

One day Toolly and Lou were off to town on the wagon. Their short conversation, as remembered by Granddaddy Rufus, went something like this:

Lou: Toolly, I will not go to town or have anything to do with anyone who uses whiskey or is around it. If you have any whiskey hidden in this wagon, either it or I have to go.

Toolly: Whoa mule. Get out of the wagon, Lou.

Again, as Granddaddy Rufus told it:

Toolly had a black helper named Zeb. (Actually the name of Toolly's helper has been lost to time. I call him Zeb because it's easy to spell.) Toolly and Zeb had been working several weeks to run one the biggest batches of moonshine they had ever done. They had amassed four thirty-gallon barrels of 'shine. Toolly was just finishing tapping in the last bung when heard Zeb come crashing and splashing through the brush and bog of the swamp.

Zeb: There is revenuers coming down the swamp on this side of the run.

Toolly: OK, Zeb you go up the swamp 'bout a hundred yards and when you see 'em, let out a whistle. Then high- tail it back to the farm.

Toolly said a little prayer: Oh Lord, if you'll only help now, I'll try to do better in the future....And with that the Spirit moved Toolly and gave him the strength, at only five foot- eight inches tall and 160 pounds, to lift, lug, and roll those four barrels weighing about 250 pounds each to a shallow depression in the swamp floor.

The Spirit moved Toolly and Toolly moved the spirits.

Toolly had just finished covering the barrels with pine and cypress needles when he heard Zeb's whistle. He made fast tracks back to the farm to keep a sharp eye out for the revenuers. None came. The next morning Toolly made his way through the swamp to his still. As expected, his still was now just a pile of junk littering the swamp floor. But, praise the Lord, his moonshine was safe under the pile of needles.

True to his word, Toolly was in church the next Sunday. He searched the Bible cover to cover and at no place in the Good Book could he find the words moonshine or whiskey. Now the part about "render unto Caesar" worried him a bit, but then he figured Caesar didn't have a still.

Authors note: This article was originally written for a publication of the Edgecombe (NC) Historical Society, *Lines and Pathways of Edgecombe County*. The research was by both authors and Margaret did the (much needed) editing and added the second through third paragraphs as best I recall. JHD

Jacob^4 Barnes (Edward^3, James^2, Thomas^1) of Southampton County, Virginia, Edgecombe, Northampton, and Pitt Counties, North Carolina,

by Joe H. Drake (Southampton County, Virginia)
and Margaret Van Ness Nelson (Powell, Ohio)
29 December 2004

Southampton County, Virginia, was a gateway south into North Carolina. Many families of North Carolina counties such as Bertie, Chowan, Edgecombe, Gates, Halifax, Hertford, Nash, Northampton, Martin and Pitt can trace their roots back to the Virginia counties of Southampton or Isle of Wight, from which Southampton was formed in 1749. The family researcher in North Carolina who finds himself or herself at a dead end, no pun intended, would do well to look in Southampton for that elusive ancestor.

Locating a document that provides new information is always a thrill for family historians. Recently, Joe Drake discovered three Northampton Co., N.C., deeds dated 1802 and 1803, with names and residences for the children of Jacob^4 Barnes. He shared this information with Margaret Nelson, thus inspiring this article.

As a resident of Southampton County, Joe Drake's perspective is particularly helpful because he is familiar with Southampton people and places. He is descended from Thomas^5 Barnes, a son of Jacob^4 and a grandson of Edward^3 Barnes of Southampton County. Margaret is descended from Martha^4 "Patsy" Barnes (a sister of Jacob^4 and a daughter of Edward^3 Barnes) who married Shadrack Vick. Margaret's perspective is helpful because she and two other Barnes descendants have published some of their Barnes research. [1], [2] Joe recently posted on the Internet a history of the Barnes Methodist Church in Southampton County, Virginia.[3]

In this article we will present abstracts of the three deeds and give a brief background on Edward^3 Barnes and his son Jacob^4 Barnes. We will summarize what the deeds helped us learn about Jacob^4's children and the land they bought and sold. Our on-going goal is to locate other descendants and/or researchers who might provide a missing piece of the puzzle.

Northampton Co., N.C., Deed Abstracts

Note that the name Evans Pope is spelled Evands in the first two deeds. Because he could not read, he probably didn't notice the difference. James made his mark with a "B" in the first two deeds and with an "X" in the third. Numerous names have varied spellings, such as Linney James, Levinia James, and James Munger, just to name a few. Perhaps some of these differences were due to the clerks who copied the documents or the way we deciphered them.

*****

Northampton Co., N.C., DB 12:79-80—Benjamin Barnes and wife Lenney, Josiah Barnes and wife Levina, Evands Pope and wife Sarah, Nancy Barnes, Thomas Barnes, and Jacob Barnes of Southampton Co., Va., likewise James Barnes and William Barnes of Edgecombe Co., N.C., to Joshua Barnes of Northampton Co, N.C. — Consideration £60 Virginia money—165 acres in Northampton Co, N.C.— bounded by Edward Saurey, William Munger, Samuel Munger, William Halley, Jeremiah Grizzard— witnesses James Mungar Junr and Michael Mungar—(signed) James (B) Barnes, Evands (x) Pope, Sarah (x) Pope, Benjamin Barnes, Linnie Barnes, Thomas Barnes, William Barnes, Jacob Barnes, Nancy Barnes, Josiah (x) Barnes, Levina Barnes—made 29 May 1802—registered 17 July 1802.

*****

Northampton Co., N.C. DB 12:80-81—Benjamin Barnes and wife Linnea, Evands Pope and wife Sarah, Josiah Barnes and wife Levina, Nancy Barnes, Thomas Barnes and Jacob Barnes of Southampton Co., Va., likewise James

Barnes and William Barnes of Edgecombe Co., N.C., to Joshua Barnes of Northampton Co., N.C.—Consideration £60 Virginia money—230 acres in Northampton Co., N.C.—bounded by the north side of Kirby's Creek, Abraham Joyner, John Bottom, Henry Suter, Piney Branch—witnesses James Mungar Junr and Michael Mungar—(signed) James (B) Barnes, Evands (x) Pope, Sarah (x) Pope, Benjamin Barnes, Linney Barnes, Thomas Barnes, William Barnes, Jacob Barnes, Nancy Barnes, Josiah (x) Barnes, Levina Barnes—made 29 May 1802—registered 19 July 1802.

*****

Northampton Co., N.C., DB 12:231-2—Benj[n] Barnes and wife Linney, Josiah Barnes and wife Levina, Evans Pope and wife Sarah, Nancy Barnes, Thomas Barnes of Southampton Co, Va., likewise James Barnes, Joshua Barnes and wife Priscilla, and William Barnes of the State of North Carolina to Jacob Barnes of Southampton Co., Va.—Consideration 160 silver dollars—148 acres in Northampton Co., N.C.— bounded by John Davis, Thomas Dupree, Jonathan Pope, Robert Parks, Wild Cat [Swamp] —witnesses Michael Mungar Junr and John Suter—(signed) James (x) Barnes, Thomas Barnes, Josiah (x) Barnes, Benjamin Barnes, Nancy Barnes, Evans (x) Pope, Sarah (x) Pope, William Barnes, Joshua Barnes—made 20 Aug1803—registered 13 June 1804.

The Children of Edward[3] and Elizabeth Barnes

1) **Jacob[4] Barnes** d. 1796 Southampton Co., VA.
2) Joshua[4] Barnes b. 1740, d. ca 1816, Pitt Co., NC.
3) James[4] Barnes b. 1718, d. 1822, Liv Co., KY.
4) Burwell[4] Barnes d. by 1777.
5) Mary[4] "Mollie" Barnes m. Edmund Barrett.
6) Priscilla[4] Barnes m. Nathan English.
7) Elizabeth[4] Barnes m. Samuel Vick.
8) Martha[4] "Patsy" Barnes m. Shadrack Vick.

Jacob[4] Barnes

Jacob[4] (ca 1735 - January 1796) was typical of many Southampton men who invested in North Carolina land—in Jacob[4]'s case in Edgecombe, Northampton and Pitt counties.

Jacob[4] was a son of Edward[3] Barnes, who was born about 1699, Isle of Wight Co., VA, and died in Southampton Co. in 1762.[4] Edward[3]'s sons were Jacob[4], Joshua[4], James[4] and Burwell[4]. Jacob[4] stayed on the home place while Joshua[4] and James[4] moved from Southampton Co. Burwell[4] died young.

Jacob[4]'s children, named in his will, were residents of Southampton Co., VA and the North Carolina counties of Pitt, Edgecombe, Hertford and Northampton. Until the discovery of the deeds, we knew few details about the children, finding it difficult to know who belonged to which of the many Barnes families in Southampton County.

The deeds helped us determine relationships among the names we found in wills, estate records, deeds and census records. Jacob[4]'s will, dated 15 Sept 1790 and proved at court 11 Feb 1796, named as executors his wife Elizabeth and his son Josiah[5].[5] In his will he left to his:

- sons Benjamin[5] and Jacob[5], land in Southampton Co.,Va.
- daughters Anne[5] Barnes and Sela[5] Vick, a room in his house while they were unmarried (Sela[5]'s surname was Vick so we concluded that she was a widow).
- sons Josiah and Thomas, Jacob[4]'s plantation and lands in Southampton Co. after their mother's death.
- sons Joshua[5] and William[5], one tract of land in Pitt Co., N.C., near Little Contenly Creek.
- son James[5], a tract of land on Hurricane branch in Edgecombe Co., N.C.

The rest was left as a life estate to his widow. If she remarried, it was to be divided equally between his wife and his children, with the home plantation going to sons Josiah[5] and Thomas[5]. The will was signed by Jacob[4] and witnessed by Edmund (E) Barrett, James Barnes, Jesse Vick, and Jesse Barrett.

Children are often named in wills by their birth order, which here would be Benjamin[5], Jacob[5], Anne[5], Sela[5], Josiah[5], Thomas[5], Joshua[5], William[5] and James[5]. However, we do not believe they followed this custom.

Benjamin^5 was probably his oldest son and Jacob^5, born in 1779, the youngest. It appears that Josiah^5 was named an executor because he was the oldest son at home. Benjamin^5 was a Methodist circuit minister, details of which may be found in the Methodist Minutes.[6]

The birth dates of the children were estimated using census and estate records, when available. Jacob^4's daughter Sarah^5 was unknown as a family member until the discovery of the Northampton deeds. Jacob^4's will did not include her, probably because she was married, and thus had no need of a room that Jacob^4 willed to Sela^5 and Anne^5.

Originally, we believed that Sela^5 and Anne^5 were the youngest children but, if Sela was a widow, maybe she was one of the older children. No guardian records have been found, which would indicate that the daughters were at least 13 and the sons 15 when their father's will was proved in 1796. An examination of the deed books reveals that the estate was not settled until 1802, at which time Jacob, assumedly the youngest, would have just turned 21. Joe Drake discussed this with Paul Drake, J.D. It is Paul's opinion that the estate was probably held open until then so that guardians need not be appointed for the younger children.

The Children of Jacob^4 and Elizabeth Barnes

1) Benjamin^5 Barnes m. Linney Lee, 1795.
2) Josiah^5 Barnes m. Lavinia Britt, 1798; 2nd Patience Oliver Sheiffield.
3) Sela^5 Barnes Vick.
4) Sarah^5 Barnes m. Evans Pope, 1787.
5) Thomas^5 Barnes m. Dorothy Drake, 1807.
6) Joshua^5 Barnes m. Priscilla, after 1803.
7) William^5 Barnes m. Susan, (Oliver?), by 1820.
8) James^5 Barnes.
9) (Nancy)^5 Anne Barnes, possibly m. 26 Apr 1805 James Newsum.
10) Jacob^5 Barnes b. 1779, d. 1856, m. Lucy Barrett 1804.

Benjamin^5 Barnes (ca. 1764-1827). In October 2004, Joe Drake posted on the Internet an article he had written about the history of the Barnes Methodist Church.[7] In response, he received two pieces of helpful information from Peggy Vaughan McKenny.

First, a marriage date and place, 22 Jan1795, Gates Co., N.C., for Benjamin^5 Barnes and his wife Linney Lee.[8] Perhaps Gates was part of the Bertie circuit for Rev. Ben? We estimate Benjamin^5's birth about 1764 and Linney's about 1780 which would make her only 15 at her marriage.

Second, a chancery record for the division of Benjamin's land, dated 21 March 1836: Linnea Barnes, defendant, versus some of Benjamin's children and grandchildren.[9]

Census Records. In *The 1787 Census of Virginia*, (a "census" based on the personal property tax records which included non-residents) Ben^5 Barnes is listed separately, although Jacob^4 is charged with the tax.[10] (In all his other census records he is Benjamin.) This indicates that Benjamin^5 was more than 21 years of age. Jacob^4's listing shows two white males between 16 and 21, no blacks, 4 horses, mares, colts and mules, and 15 cattle.[11] No such information is given for Ben^5.

There are two Benjamin Barnes in the 1810 census. The first was16-26 years old, with neighbors that included Henry O'Berry and Thomas Johnson, both well known to have lived in Nottoway Parish on the east side of Nottoway Swamp.[12] Thus, this is not 46-year-old Benjamin, son of Jacob^4, in St. Luke's Parish.

The other Benjamin had neighbors Reuben Whitfield and Dixon Ferguson.[13] This places his residence around what today is known as the Sunbeam-Mt. Horeb area, close to other Barnes families. In this census, Benjamin was 45 + and Linney, 26-45 with three males under 10, two males 10-16, one female under 10, one female 10-16, and one female 16-26.

In the 1820 census, only one Benjamin was enumerated.[14] This household had two males under 10, two males 10-15, two males 15-18, two males 18-26, and one male over 45, plus two females under 10, one female 15-26, and one female 26-45.

Linney, but not Benjamin, was listed as the head of household in the 1830 census of Southampton with males 10-14 and 15-19 and females 10-14, 15-19, and 40-49.[15] An account current for Benjamin Barnes indicates that he died intestate in 1827. Possibly one of his last real estate transactions was a deed of trust, from Benjamin Worrell to Benjamin Barnes, dated 20 Nov 1826. Benjamin Barnes appointed his brothers Thomas and Jacob as trustees.[16]

Barnes Church. Oddly, while Benjamin[5] was a founder and one of the first five trustees of Barnes Methodist Church,[17] he was not listed as being the minister there from 1808 forward. Records of the ministers who served prior to 1808 have not been found to date.[18] Perhaps in 1803, as it is today, it was a conflict of interest for a trustee to also serve as the minister.

The church was built on one acre of land that Jacob[5] Barnes sold for $1 to the trustees of the church: Benjamin Barrett, Benjamin Barnes, Exum Everett, Nathan Britt and Evans Pope. (At that time in Virginia, $1 was the minimum consideration to legally bind a deed.) The deed was signed by Jacob[5] Barnes and witnessed by Reuben Whitfield, Pilgrim Vick, Lucy Barrett and Betsey Whitehead, surnames found often in Barnes documents.[19]

Children. Two children of Benjamin[5] Barnes, sons John[6] E. Barnes, and Jacob[6] D. Barnes, both of whom moved to Iowa, were named in the will of Benjamin[5]'s brother Jacob[5].[20]

The others identified were in the Chancery suit, such as his son Robert S. Barnes, who served as an associate minister of Barnes Methodist Church for more than 30 years.[21] He lived close to, if not on, the farm owned by Benjamin[5]. Jacob Barnes was the surety for Robert's marriage bond in 1829.[22] In addition to performing marriages, Robert was a frequent witness to family deeds and wills.

Children identified to date:

Richard[6] Barnes, son Richard[7] Barnes.
Benjamin[6] H. Barnes, son Benjamin[7] Barnes.
Robert[6] S. Barnes, b. 1804, wife Matilda Worrell, d/o Temperance and Lewis Worrell.[23] Six children.
Martha F. Barnes.
John E. Barnes.
Marmaduke[6] N. Barnes, b. betw 1810-1820, m. Jane S. McMains, 14 Nov 1837, Putnam County, IN. Six children.
Mary[6] Barnes, m. Edmund Garrett and had children Maria[7] and William[7].
Jacob[6] Davis Barnes, b. ca 1820, m. Catherine McMains, 6 Dec 1846, Putnam County, IN. Four daughters.

Josiah[5] (ca. 1767 – after 1832). Josiah[5] may have been the second oldest child and was probably the oldest son living at home in 1790 when named an executor of his father's will. He and his brother Thomas[5] were left a reversionary interest to the home plantation after the death of their mother, Elizabeth. He sold his interest to Thomas[5] in 1803,[24] which would seem to indicate that his mother had died. The Northampton deeds are another indication of Elizabeth's death, as the deeds would have been unspecified property, which the older Jacob left to his wife.

However, an inventory and appraisement for Elizabeth Barnes was taken 3 June 1813, by William Barnes administrator, Jacob Barrett, Lewis Worrell and Jordan Barrett appraisers, and recorded August, 1816.[25] The record was followed by an Account Current for Elizabeth Barnes, Executrix of Jacob Barnes dec'd. Although it is 13 years after her death, it is possible that this could still be Elizabeth, wife of the older Jacob. For some reason, this family never seemed to be in any hurry to settle estates.

Josiah[5] married Levinia Britt, 18 June 1798, by consent of her guardians, Arthur and Sally Whitehead.[26] Levinia was not yet 21. If she was 18 at marriage (thus 13 years younger than her husband) she was born in 1780. One Britt researcher believes Levinia was an orphan whose father might have been Jesse or John Britt.

Joe Drake notes that Jesse and John were both sons of Nathan Britt, one of the first trustees of Barnes Church. Jesse, who spelled his name most often with an "e" rather than an "ie", was Joe's great-great- great grandfather. Jesse married Sidney Everett, daughter of Exum Everett, also one of the first trustees of Barnes Church. Many relationships seemed to revolve around Barnes Church.

In his will, dated 1811 and recorded in 1815, Nathan made provisions for Jordan Britt, son of his son John, but not for John.[27] Perhaps John died before his father. Levinia was probably a daughter of John considering that Jesse was alive at the time of her marriage.

In 1806 Josiah Barnes sold 50 acres in Northampton Co., N.C., for £37, 10 shillings Virginia money, to Jesse Britt of Southampton Co., Virginia.[28] This could have been Levinia's uncle.

The Northampton deeds indicate that Josiah[5] and Levinia were living in Southampton in 1802 and1803.[29] By 13 Jan 1806, when he sold the land to Jesse Britt, Josiah was a Northampton Co. resident. Josiah was listed in the 1810 census, Northampton Co., as 26-45 with one male under 10, one male 10-16, one female under ten and one female 26-45.[30] In the 1820 census, Northampton Co., N.C., he was age 45+, thus born 1775 or earlier.[31] In the 1830 census, a male aged 70-80 lived with William[6] B. Barnes, Josiah[5]'s son. This could be Josiah[5], born 1750-60,[32] in which case he would be older than Benjamin[5].

Three children of Josiah[5] and Levinia Britt were named in the will of their uncle Jacob[5]: William[6], Samuel[6], and Elizabeth[6].[33] Another, Jacob[6], was named as a brother of Samuel[6] and William[6] in a Southampton County Chancery Suit in 1868.[34]

We believe that Levinia Britt died before 1817 when Josiah[5] married Patience (Oliver) Sheiffield, the widow of Josiah Sheiffield.[35] David B. Gammon's *Records of Estates* shows the administration was granted to James Oliver at Dec Court 1813, and a year's provisions allotted to the widow Patience Shuffield [*sic*] in 1813 and 1814. The estate was settled in Dec court 1815.[36] Josiah Sheiffield's estate records shows James Oliver, Josiah Oliver and Israel Martin posted a £500 bond, dated 6 Dec 1813, and James Oliver was the administrator of the estate.[37] A Northampton Co., N.C., deed, made 6 March 1820 and recorded 4 April 1823, lists Josiah Barnes and wife Patience.[38]

In 1832, Josiah[5] Barnes sold 173 acres for $140 to [his sons, but not so named in the deed] William[6] B. and Samuel[6] E. Barnes.[39] Josiah bought the 173 acres from Thomas Sikes/Sykes in 1815 for $389.25.[40]

Children:

- William[6] B. Barnes, b. ca. 1802, wife Martha Edwards.[41]
- Samuel[6] E. Barnes, b. ca. 1806, wife Sidney E.
- Elizabeth[6] Barnes, b. ca. 1800-1809, married a Lane.
- Jacob[6] Barnes.

Sela[5] Barnes (ca. 1768 –before 1801). Sela[5] was left a right to a room in Jacob[4]'s house until she married. According to the book *Joseph Vick of Lower Parish, Isle of Wight County, Virginia and his Descendants, Vol. 1,* Selah [*sic*] Barnes married Jesse Vick (born 1755-60, d. before 18 July 1818), although no documentation is given.[42] Jesse did witness Jacob[4] Barnes's will but was not his son-in-law as the Vick book maintains. The editors, John Beatty and Di An Vick, have recently agreed that Sela probably was the widow of a yet unidentified Vick. The fact that the Northampton County deeds name all the siblings except Sela[5] suggests that she died without issue before 1802. However, the name Selah [*sic*] Vick appeared in the 1827-28 Account Current of Benjamin[5].[43] More research is needed to determine if this was the daughter of Jacob[4].

Sarah[5] (ca. 1769–d. after 1830 but before 1840). Sarah[5] was positively identified as a child of Jacob[4] and Elizabeth by the three Northampton deeds. We assume that she was not mentioned in her father's will because she was married and had no need for the life right to a room.

Sarah[5] married (Benjamin) Evans Pope on 30 Jan 1787 by the consent of her parents, Elizabeth and Jacob Barnes, indicating that Sarah[5] was not yet 21.[44] Sarah[5]'s age at her marriage is estimated at 18, thus a birth year of 1769.

The 1810 census shows the Evans Pope household with one male over 45, one female less than 10, one female 16-26, and one female 26-45.[45] In 1820 there was one male over 45, one female under 10, one female 15-26 and one female over 45.[46] Evans Pope died in March 1828.[47] Sarah[5]'s death date is unknown.

The children of Evans Pope and Sarah[5] Barnes were named in the will of Evans Pope.

Children:

- Joseph[6] Pope, d. December 1829, married Sally.
- Sally[6] Pope, 10 November1802- 11 Mar1851, married Alexander Myrick.
- Elizabeth[6] Pope, 22 September 1790–6 January1857, married 1st Beale and 2nd Miles Story.

Thomas[5] (ca.1770 – 1836). Thomas[5] and his brother Josiah[5] received a reversionary interest in the home plantation.[48] Thomas[5] purchased his brother's interest in 1803.[49] Like his brother Jacob[5], Thomas[5] dealt frequently in real estate. He is mentioned in no fewer than twelve Southampton deeds as the grantor, grantee, or trustee. He and brother Jacob^{5} used each other as trustee on deeds of trust that served as security on money they lent or land they sold and financed.

In 1800 Thomas^{5} fathered a child out of wedlock with Dorothy Drake (also known as Dora, or Dorcy), daughter of Jesse and Ann Drake. In April 1805, Dorothy sued Thomas^{5} for what today would be called child support for their daughter Dorothy^{6} (Doary, or Dory).[50] The case was continued and no decision in the case has been found. Evidently the case was dropped when Thomas^{5} promised to marry Dorothy, which he did in March of 1807, at the age of 37 or 38 years.[51] Their daughter Dorothy^{6} (named for her mother), born about 1800, was the only child of their union.

To continue with the confusion of the names Dorothy and Thomas, it appears that the child Dorothy^{6} also had at least one child born out of wedlock, a daughter, Elizabeth^{7}, who carried the surname Barnes. Dorothy^{6} later married Thomas Drake (tentatively identified as a son of Drewry and Sarah Kitchen Drake), by whom she had two sons: William^{7} and James^{7} E. Drake. At James^{7} E. Drake's death in 1859, his widow Susan Edwards Drake named his parents as Thomas and Dorothy Drake. Dorothy^{6}'s three children could account for the younger people in Thomas Barnes^{5}'s household in the 1810, 1820 and 1830 census records.

William^{7} and James^{7} are important to this tale for three reasons. First, they inherited the home plantation of Old Jacob^{4}. Second, they are mentioned in the will of Jacob^{5}, the only grandnephews so named. Third, they help reveal the occasionally difficult character of Jacob^{5}, who left out the grandchildren of his sister Sarah^{5} (Benjamin^{6} E. and Harrison^{6} P. Pope)—possibly because he disapproved of their business dealings with William^{7} and James^{7} Drake, believing that the Popes were unduly harsh in their treatment of William^{7} and James^{7}. Jacob^{5} had guaranteed the debts of William^{7} and James^{7} E. Drake to Benjamin^{7} E. and Harrison^{7} P. Pope in 1852.

Thomas left a will, made 9 Aug 1836 and proved 19 Dec 1836, which does not mention a wife.[52] Thus Dorothy, listed in the 1830 census, must have died before 1836. Thomas Barnes left his daughter Dorothy^{6} a life right to his house. He left the balance of his sizable estate to be divided between his three grandchildren: Elizabeth^{7} Barnes, William^{7} Drake, and James^{7} E. Drake. Reversionary interest in the house was left to William^{7}.

Children:

Dorothy^{6} Barnes, married Thomas Drake.

<u>Joshua</u>^{5} (ca. 1771 – 1816?). Joshua^{5}, along with his brother William^{5}, was left land in Pitt Co., N.C., which they later sold to Joshua^{4} Barnes Sr., undoubtedly their uncle, a Primitive Baptist minister in Pitt County.[53] Their brothers Jacob^{5} and Thomas^{5} were witnesses for the sale.

In 1802 Joshua^{5} and his wife Priscilla (possibly the daughter of neighbor Samuel Mungar of Northampton Co., N.C.)[54] lived in Northampton Co., N.C., where Joshua^{5} bought two of the three properties as noted in the Northampton Co. deeds cited earlier. The state and county line for Northampton Co. are within five miles of Old Jacob^{4}'s home place, while Hertford Co. is within two miles. So, while dealing with three counties in two states, the distances involved are relatively short.

Joshua^{5} could be the one in the 1810 Hertford Co., N.C. census.[55] Priscilla could be the one in the 1820 census in Hertford Co., N.C.[56] The 1830 Hertford Co. census lists a Jacob Barnes with a female in the 60-69 year old range. This could be Priscilla living with her son.[57]

In 1816, in Southampton Co., an inventory for a Joshua Barnes was taken by John Kitchen, Jesse J. West and James West. Joshua had only two trunks, one "toket" book, one testament, one "cyphering book," one razor and one parcel.[58] This was not a prosperous estate as we would expect of Jacob^{4}'s son but no other estate records have been located there or in Northampton Co., N.C.

Priscilla Barnes died in 1843. In her will in Southampton Co., she named children James^{6} M., Jacob^{6}, Elizabeth^{6} M. (maybe for Mungar?) Everett and Sally^{6} H. Everett. Son Jacob^{6} was the executor.[59] James^{6} and Jacob^{6} were also named in the will of their uncle Jacob^{5}.[60] The 1850 census record for Thomas and Sally Everitt [*sic*] gives her age as 43, born in North Carolina. Thus the family lived there in1807.

Children:

James^{6} M. Barnes, m. Lydia W. Beale.
Jacob^{6} Barnes, m. Caroline (Ellsworth?).
Elizabeth^{6} M. Barnes, m. Burwell Everett.
Sally^{6} H. Barnes, b. ca. 1807, m. Thomas Everett.

Dau Martha Francis Everett Barrett (1844-1926),
wife of Richard Alexander Barrett (1833-1881),
son of Henry and Julia Barrett.

William^5 (ca.1775 – May 1847). William^5 and his brother Joshua^5 were left property in Pitt Co., N.C., as noted above. At the time of the Northampton deeds, 1802 and 1803, William^5 and his brother James^5 were residents of Edgecombe Co., N.C. Those deeds exhibit no dower considerations for William^5 or James^5.

Several Northampton deeds after 1803 involve a William Barnes who has yet to be identified. There is one Southampton Co. deed that does involve this William^5. It is the 100 acre farm previously owned by Mary Vick Pope who ,before she died, sold it to her nephew, Newit Vick, who sold it to William Barnes.[61]

The William Barnes listed in the 1810 census is over 45 with children and in Nottoway Parish.[62] This is not the William^5 Barnes, son of Old Jacob^4.

There is no William Barnes listed in the index of the 1820 census for Southampton Co., although William^5 had owned property in the county for at least six years. William^5 is in the 1830 census as 50-60 years old with one female 40-50, probably his wife Susan.[63]

The 1840 Southampton Co. census for William^5's household shows one male 60-70 (William), one female 40-50 (unknown) and one female 50-60 (Susan).[64]

William^5 died in 1847, dividing his farm into a 25-acre tract he left to Susan as a life estate and a 75-acre tract he left to brother Jacob^5 in exchange for caring for Susan.[65] Receiving a reversionary interest to the tract left to Susan and his personal property were James^6 and Jacob^6 (sons of his brother Joshua^5), Robert^6 S. Barnes (son of his brother Benjamin^5), and Benjamin^7 E. Pope and Harrison^7 P. Pope (grandsons of his sister Sarah^5 by her son Joseph^6 Pope). The will of Evans Pope names his son Joseph^6[66] who died just a year after his father. And the will of Joseph^6 Pope names his sons Benjamin^7 E. and Harrison^7 P.[67]

William^5 and Susan had no children.

James^5 (ca. 1776 – ?). Very little is known about James^5. His father left him property in Edgecombe Co., N.C., where he was living in 1802 and 1803, according to Northampton Co. deeds. No spouse was given for him. There were two other James Barnes in the Southampton Co. census records for 1820 and 1830, but these seem to be in Nottoway Parish, rather than St. Luke's Parish, where Jacob resided.

Anne^5 (ca. 1777 –?). Anne^5 was unmarried and living at home when her father died and he left her a room in the homeplace. The Northampton deeds listed her as a resident of Southampton County. There was a marriage between Nancy Barnes and James Newsom 26 April 1805.[68] Nancy was a common nickname for Anne, so this may have been Jacob^4's daughter. In the census of 1810, James is listed as being 26-45 with two females under 10 and one female 26-45.[69] No other records have been located.

Jacob^5 (1779—1856). Jacob^5's legacy was a farm adjoining the homeplace. He is the one child of Old Jacob^4 with a death record. In 1856, his nephew James^6 (son of Joshua^5) knew his age, 77, but not the names of Jacob^5's parents.[70]

While Jacob^5 always gave his occupation as farmer, in reality he was what today would be called an investment banker and real estate speculator. Jacob^5 was either a grantor or grantee in many Southampton Co. deeds. Only a few of these have been examined to date. He also had deeds in Northampton Co., N.C., and probably had deeds in Hertford Co., but that courthouse was burned in 1862.

In 1803, Jacob^5 donated one acre in Southampton County for the Barnes Methodist Church.[71] Reading between the lines, we surmise that he may have been coerced by his older brother, the Reverend Benjamin^5 Barnes, or his brother-in-law Evans Pope, or the man who would become his father-in-law the next year, Benjamin Barrett. These men were three of the first five trustees of the church. No record has been found of Jacob^5 ever being a member of the church that bears his name.

In an 1804 marriage service by Rev. Benjamin^5 Barnes, Jacob^5 wed Lucy Barrett, daughter of Rev. Benjamin and Catherine Barnes Barrett.[72] The surety was Thomas^5 Barnes. No census records indicate that Jacob^5 and Lucy had children and he names no children in his will.[73]

Jacob[5]'s lengthy will has been helpful in naming some of his siblings' children. Part of his character is revealed by an often over-looked sentence near the beginning of his will that states he has made no provisions for anyone with whom he had discord within the last year. We know he left nothing to his niece Dorothy[6] Barnes Drake, daughter of Thomas[5], although he did remember her two sons William[7] and James[7] E. Drake, as well as James's[7]' son Thomas[8] Drake. These grand-nephews were also Jacob[5]'s closest neighbors, owning and living on the plantation that had belonged to Old Jacob[4]. He left nothing to Jacob[6], son of his brother Josiah[5], nor to any of the offspring of his sister Sarah[5] Pope nor to Robert[6] S. Barnes.

The Northampton Land

The 543 acres involved in the three deeds were located near the Southampton Co., Virginia and North Carolina border. Jacob[4] purchased the165 acres from Hayley Burt for £100 in a deed dated 2 April 1795 and registered in Sept Court 1795 not long before Jacob died. Witnesses for the deed were Edward Sawreys and Hullen Grizzard. The siblings sold this land to Joshua[5] Barnes. How Jacob[4] Barnes acquired the other 378 acres is yet unknown.

Joshua and Jacob quickly sold the land they purchased from their siblings. Joshua sold his 165 acres to William Faison for £120 in a deed dated 16 Sept 1803 and registered 3 May 1804[74], making a profit of £60. Joshua sold the other 230 acres, which he bought for £60, to James Mungar for £195. Jacob[5] sold his tract to Benjamin Railey [Raleigh] on 5 Nov1804.[75] He financed it naming Thomas[5] as trustee. He bought it back at auction from Trustee Thomas[5] on 20 Nov1806[76] and resold it to Arthur Davis on 1 Jan1808[77].

Conclusion.

Tracing the descendants of Edward[3] Barnes through his Southampton County offspring is a challenge because Barnes is a common surname and the names Benjamin, James, Jacob and Joshua were common among Barnes families.

Therefore, the three Northampton Co., N.C., deeds provided useful, new information. Researching everything connected to these deeds, we learned that:

1. Jacob[4] Barnes bought land, including 543 acres in Northampton Co., N.C., between 1790, when he made his will, and 1796 when he died.
2. Because Jacob[4]'s wife Elizabeth and daughter Sela[5] Vick were not mentioned in the deeds, we concluded that they died before 1802. However, the name Selah [*sic*] Vick appeared in the Account Current of Benjamin[5]. Also there was an estate for Elizabeth Barnes settled in 1813. More research is needed here.
3. Sarah[5] Barnes, who married Evans Pope, was a daughter of Jacob[4].
4. Peggy Vaughan McKenny provided us with the marriage record of Benjamin[5] and Linney Lee and with records for two of their sons, Marmaduke[6] Barnes and Jacob[6] Davis Barnes.
5. Joshua[5]'s wife was Patience (probably Oliver).
6. Nancy[5], Thomas[5], William[5], Jacob[5] and James[5] were not married by 1803.
7. William[5]'s wife, Susannah, was probably an Oliver.
8. Josiahs[5]'s wife, Priscilla, may have been a Munger/Mungar.
9. William[5] and James[5] lived in Edgecombe Co., N.C., in 1802.
10. Thomas[5] lived in Southampton Co. in 1803.
11. Jacob[5], Benjamin[5] and Linney, Josiah[5] and Levinia, Sarah[5] and Evans Pope, and Nancy[5] lived in Southampton Co. in 1802.
12. All but Josiah[5], Patience and James[5] Barnes, Evans and Sarah[5] Pope could sign their names.

The deeds served as a guide as we sorted through wills, estate, and land records. We share our research with hopes that it will help locate other descendants or that other researchers might be able to provide a missing piece of the puzzle.

---

[1] Margaret Van Ness Nelson, with Research Assistance by Barbara Barnes Monroe and Carol LaPorte, "Which Edward Barnes Was the Son of James, Isle of Wight County, Virginia?" *Lines and Pathways of Edgecombe County* volume 5 (Jan 2001): 4-8. Reprint of Edward Barnes article from *Trees of Wilson.*

---

[2] Margaret Van Ness Nelson, with Research Assistance by Barbara Barnes Monroe and Carol LaPorte, "Reverend Joshua Barnes' Connections to the Bynum and Davis Families and Others: Edgecombe and Pitt Counties, North Carolina," *Lines and Pathways of Edgecombe County* volume 5(April 2001): 5-10.
[3] Yahoo Groups, Southamptonhistory, file. Must be a member to access site.
[4] Edward Barnes will (1762), Southampton Co., VA, WB 1: 441-3, County Clerk's Office, Courtland, VA. Edward Barnes's will, dated 15 July 1761 and proved 11 March 1762, Southampton Co., VA, names his wife Elizabeth, his sons Jacob (executor), Joshua, James, and Burwell, and his daughters Mary Barrett, Priscilla, Elizabeth and Martha.[4] Edward signed the will with his mark. Witnesses were Epahroditus (x) Williams, Richard Kemp, and Richard Vick.
[5] Jacob Barnes will (1796) Southampton Co., VA, WB 4: 723, County Clerk's Office, Courtland, VA.
[6] *The Minutes of the Conferences –1773-1813. Vol. 1.* New York: Published by Daniel Hitt and Thomas Ware. (From Methodist Archives, McGraw Library, Randolph-Macon College, Ashland, VA).
[7] Yahoo Groups, Southamptonhistory, file.
[8] Gates County, North Carolina, Marriage Bonds, typed by the Genealogical Society of Utah, 80 N. Main St. Salt Lake City, UT, 1943, p. 8. Benjamin Barnes (of Southampton Co., VA) to Linney Lee 22 Jan 1795, Bondsman & Witness, Wm Baker.
[9] Southampton Co., VA, Order Book 1819-1839, p.70.
[10] Ben Barnes, The 1787 Census of Virginia, Vol. 2, p. 1127, line 9, Springfield, Virginia: Genealogical Books in Print, 1987.
[11] Jacob Barnes, The 1787 Census of Virginia, Vol. 2, p. 1127, line 8, Springfield, VA: Genealogical Books in Print, 1987.
[12] Benjamin Barnes household, 1810 U.S. census, Southampton Co., VA, page 65A, line 11. National Archives microfilm M 252, roll 71.
[13] Benjamin Barnes household, 1810 U.S. census, Southampton Co., VA, page 55A, line 18, National Archives microfilm M 252, roll 71.
[14] Benjamin Barnes household, 1820 U.S. census, Southampton Co., VA, p. 111, line 31, National Archives microfilm M33, roll 142.
[15] Linna Barnes household, 1830 U.S. census, Southampton Co., VA, p. 248, line 23, National Archives microfilm M19, roll 196.
[16] Southampton Co., VA DB 23:144, County Clerk's Office, Courtland, VA.
[17] Southampton Co., VA DB 10: 119.
[18] Betty Darden, *Historical Record Barnes United Methodist Church*, p. 7. Privately printed, 2003, for the bicentennial of the church.
[19] Southampton Co., VA, DB 10: 119, made 22 Jan 1803, recorded 19 July 1803.
[20] Jacob Barnes Will (1857), Southampton Co., VA, WB 15:667-672, FHL microfilm # 34,001.
[21] Darden, *Historical Record Barnes United Methodist Church*, p. 7.
[22] Southampton Co., VA, Marriage Bond Register, p. 404, p. 8, Robert Barnes/Matilda Worrell, 17 Jan 1829: Jacob Barnes.
[23] Northampton Co., N.C., DB 28: 98, Report of the joint commission to divide the estate of Lewis Worrell, recorded 20 July1834.
[24] Southampton Co., VA, DB 10:204-5, FHL microfilm 34009. Josiah Barnes and Levinia his wife of Southampton Co., VA to Thomas Barnes of the same—Consideration £145 Current money of Virginia —100 acres —Tract of land in Southampton Co., VA, that was conveyed to us by will of Jacob Barnes dec'd, where the said Thomas Barnes now lives— Bounded by Benjamin Barrett, Jordan Barrett, Reuben Whitfield, Benjamin Barnes, Jacob Barnes— Witnesses: Elisha Atkinson, Benj. B., Exum Vick—Signed Josiah (x) Barnes his mark, Levinia (x) Barnes, her mark—Levinia privily examined as the law directs—Dated 19 Dec 1803—Recorded 19 Dec 1803.
[25] Elizabeth Barnes Inventory (1813) Southampton Co, VA, WB 8: 161-2. FHL microfilm # 33998.
[26] Southampton Co., VA, Marriage Bond Register, page 121
[27] Nathan Britt will (1815), Southampton Co., VA, WB 7:436.
[28] Northampton Co., N.C., DB13: 127, State Archives microfilm C.071.40005.
[29] Northampton County, N.C., DB 12:79-80 and 231.

[30] Josiah Barnes household, 1810 U.S. census, Northampton Co., N.C., p. 61, line 6, National Archives microfilm 252, roll 42.
[31] Josiah Barnes household, 1820 U.S. census, Northampton Co., N.C., p. 218, line 20, National Archives microfilm 33, roll 55.
[32] William B. Barnes household, 1830 U.S. census, Northampton Co., N.C., p. 123a, line 13, National Archives microfilm 19, roll 123.
[33] Southampton Co., VA, WB 15: 667-672.
[34] Southampton Co., VA, Chancery Order Book 1859-1882, page 145.
[35] Southampton Co., VA, Marriage Bond Register, p. 257. Josiah Barnes and Patience Sheiffield, 11 April 1817. Surety William Barnes
[36] David B. Gammon, *Record of Estate Northampton County, N.C.*, Vol. 2. Estates found in Court Records 1792-1816, (Raleigh, N.C.: David B. Gammon, 1988), p. 81, # 897.
[37] Josiah Sheffield estate (1813), Northampton Co., N.C., Estate Records 1785-1929, State Archives 071.508.183.
[38] Northampton Co., N.C., Deed Book 20: 319, made 6 March 1820, recorded 4 April 1823. Grantors: Josiah Barnes and Patience, his wife, John Oliver, Joseph Oliver, James Oliver, William Barnes and Suzannah, his wife, William Oliver, Edmund Thorp and Mary his wife. (Edmund was the brother of Margaret Nelson's ancestor Joshua Thorp, sons of John Thorp and Charity Barrett, d/o Edmund Barrett who witnessed Old Jacob[4]'s will.)
[39] Northampton Co., N.C., DB 25:396, made 3 March 1832, recorded 31 March 1832. Josiah Barnes to William B. and Samuel E. Barnes, 173 acres, $140, to be equally divided between them,
[40] Northampton Co., N.C., Deed Book 17: 160
[41] Frances T. Ingmire, *Northampton County, N.C. Marriage records, 1812-1857*, p. 3. William B. Barnes and Martha Edwards, married 2 March 1829.
[42] John D. Beatty and Di An Vick, editors, *Joseph Vick of Lower Parish, Isle of Wight County, Virginia and his Descendants, Vol. 1.* (Los Angeles: Genus Publishing, 2004), p.86.
[43] Southampton Co., VA, WB 10:174-5.
[44] Evans Pope and Sarah Barns, 30 Jan 1787. Bond: Jacob & Elizabeth Barnes, parents Southampton Co., VA Marriage Bond Register, p. 170.
[45] Evans Pope household, 1810 U.S. census, Southampton Co., VA, page 59b, line 7, National Archives microfilm M 252, roll 71.
[46] Evans Pope household, 1820 U. S. census, Southampton Co., VA, page 124a, line 14, National Archives microfilm M 19, roll 196.
[47] Evans Pope will (1828), Southampton Co., VA, WB 10:85, County Clerk's Office, Courtland, VA.
[48] Southampton Co., VA, W B 4: 723.
[49] Southampton Co., VA, DB 10:204-5, FHL microfilm #34009.
[50] Southampton Co., VA, Order Book 1803-1805, entry dated April 1805.
[51] Southampton Co., VA, Marriage record, p. 178. Thomas Barnes to Dorothy Drake 16 Mar 1807. Surety: Exum Vick. Wit. Benjamin Cobb.
[52] Thomas Barnes will (1836), Southampton Co., VA, WB 11:517, FHL microfilm # 33,999.
[53] Pitt Co., N.C., DB O: 382. Deed from Joshua Barnes Jr. and William Barnes to Joshua Barnes, Senr of Pitt Co., Province of North Carolina—for £129 10 shillings lawful money of the state—516 acre tract adjoining Solomon Ward—being part of a patent granted Samuel Davis senior bearing date 11 April 1780—sold to Jacob Barnes—willed to Joshua Barnes Jr. & William Barnes—witnesses: Jacob Barnes, Thomas Barnes —(signed) Joshua Barnes & William Barnes—dated 7 Nov 1799—recorded Jan Court 1800— George Evans cc.
[54] Margaret M. Hofmann, *Northampton County, North Carolina, 1759-1808: Genealogical Abstracts of Wills* (Weldon, N.C.: Roanoke News Company, 1975), 113. Will Book 2: 228, Will of Samuel Mungar, made 1 Sept 1801, proved at Dec Court 1801. The will names Priscilla Barnes as one of his daughters.
[55] Joshua Barnes household, 1810 U.S. census, Hertford Co., N.C., p. 212, line 12, National Archives microfilm M 252, roll 40.
[56] Pricilla Barnes household, 1820 U.S. census, Hertford Co., N.C., p. 202, line 28, National Archives microfilm 33, roll85.

[57] Jacob Barnes household, 1830 U.S. census, Hertford Co., N.C., p. 402, line 6. National Archives microfilm M 19, roll 121.
[58] Joshua Barnes Account Current (1816) Southampton Co., VA, WB 9: 86-7. Joshua Barnes Inventory (1816) Southampton County WB 9: 98.
[59] Priscilla Barnes will (1843) Southampton Co., VA, WB 13: 157
[60] Southampton Co., VA, WB 15:667.
[61] Southampton Co., VA, DB 14: 243. Made Aug. 17, 1814, recorded Nov. 15, 1814. Newit Vick and Elizabeth his wife, of Warren County Territory of Mississippi, to William Barnes, $160, tract in Southampton Co., VA, on which Mary Pope, decd, formerly lived containing 100 acres. Bounded by Prickley Ash Branch, William Vick, the Fish Road, William Fowler, Simon Barrett, boundaries designated by the will of William Vick, Sr. dated 1771. Witness John Jenkins, Burwell Vick.
[62] William Barnes household, 1810 U.S. census, Southampton Co., VA, p. 146. line 7. National Archives microfilm M 252, roll 71.
[63] William Barnes household, 1830 U.S. census, Southampton Co., VA, p. 253, line 2, National Archives microfilm M19, roll 196.
[64] William Barnes household, 1840 U.S. census, Southampton Co., VA, p. 90, line 1, National Archives microfilm M704, roll 575.
[65] William Barnes will (1847) Southampton Co., VA, WB 14: 185. FHL microfilm #34,000.
[66] Southampton Co., VA, WB 10:85.
[67] Joseph Pope will (1829), Southampton Co., VA, WB 10:149, County Clerk's Office, Courtland, VA.
[68] Southampton Co., VA Marriage Bond Register, page 166.
[69] James Newsom household, 1810 U.S. census, Southampton Co., VA, p. 75 (online), line 22, National Archives microfilm M 252, roll 71.
[70] Jacob Barnes, Southampton Co., VA, Death Register, page 56.
[71] Southampton Co., VA, Deed Book 10: 119.
[72] Catherine Lindsay Knorr, *Marriage Bond and Minister's Returns of Southampton County, Virginia 1750-1810.* (Pinebluff Arkansas: The Perdue Company Duplicating Service, 1955), 6.
[73] Southampton Co., VA, WB 15: 667.
[74] Northampton Co., N.C., DB 12:207.
[75] Northampton Co., N.C., DB 12:363.
[76] Northampton Co., N.C., DB 13:243
[77] Northampton Co., N.C., DB 13:377

The Search for
Nathan Britt (or Brett)
And the Discovery

By Joe H. Drake
Researched by Joyce Britt Dunning and Joe H. Drake

Introduction:

The search for the Britt/Brett family of Southeast Virginia and Northeast North Carolina is far from finished. When the definitive book of the family is finally written, it will probably encompass several volumes. But, as my first employer (God rest his soul) would remind me about once a week, "no man is promised tomorrow". With that in mind, this essay is to shed a bit of light on just one aspect of the family that has baffled researchers for decades in hopes that it will not become obscured again for those researchers who follow – ***Who were the parents of Nathan Britt, who died in 1815 in Southampton County, Virginia, and from where did they come?***

The author gratefully acknowledges the contributions of Dot Barnum, who alerted him to the existence of the Northampton Deeds of Nathan and his brothers and supplied, along with other notes, the abstracts of some of those deeds.

And, of course, the efforts of Joyce Britt Dunning (the youngest 80 year old I have ever encountered) need to be recognized for, without her research and counsel, the Nathan problem would not have been unraveled. {Author's note: I think I wrote this narrative circa 2010-2012. Since that time Joyce has passed on. She was a driving force when it came to genealogy. Joyce Britt Dunning will be greatly missed.}

The Legend: Fact or Myth

We know that Nathan Brett died in Southampton County, Virginia sometime just before March 20, 1815, the date his will was recorded in Southampton Will Book 7, page 436. We know from the will that Nathan had a wife, Elizabeth, and four sons and four daughters. Descendants of those eight children can now be found in nearly every corner of the country. We can find deeds in Southampton showing he owned the land he passed on to his sons. Little more is factually known of the Nathan who died in 1815.

Susan (Sue) McLaughan Brett was a Brett family researcher of some renown. She was descended from Nathan's (d.1815) son John and wife Mary Liles – who were Sue's great-grandparents. Before Sue died in 1990 at the age of 88, she relayed a family legend to Joyce Britt Dunning that she had been trying to prove. Sue's aunt, Missouri Brett Taylor, her father Henan's sister, had said that they were descended from two Nathans and one of them made bells. Further, Sue stated that the tale was handed down from her grandfather's only sister. That would have been Nancy Brett Gatling, a daughter of John and Mary Liles Brett.

In genealogy, few things are less reliable than family legend; however, with this legend came a line of descent in the telling. The bad news is that Nancy Brett Gatling was born several years after her Grandfather Nathan died; therefore, she was relaying hear-say. Also, how often does one encounter bell makers in the records?

Nathans Everywhere

In his will written in 1811 (recorded 1815), Nathan referred to himself as "senior" to distinguish himself from his son Nathan, also known as Nathan, Jr. Southampton County, Virginia records involving a Nathan Brett (or Britt) seem to begin with a March, 1773, patent for land in Southampton very near the Virginia/North Carolina line (patent book 41, page 265). The records continue until November of 1821 when Nathan divided his property by deed between his wife and children. During those 48 years, the names Nathan, Nathan Sr., and Nathan, Jr. appear in no less than 24 Southampton deeds and 8 tax lists. The names Nathan, Sr. and Nathan, Jr. appear together in no less than 7 deeds either as witnesses or in which they exchanged properties (usually from Sr. to Jr.).

All this seems fairly straight forward until one does the math. Analysis of the ages of the children of the Nathan who died in 1815 would seem to suggest that his offspring were born between about 1775 and 1795. This is based on the fact that two of Nathan's daughters were under the age of 21 at the time of their marriage and required their parent's consent to wed: Rhoda who married Robert Gilliam in 1803 (Southampton Marriage Bond Register page 339) and Cherry who wed Luten Jones in 1810 (Southampton Marriage Bond Register page 210). As for Nathan, Jr., we can assume he was probably the oldest as he was named executor of his father's will along with brother William Gatling Brett. We have a confirmed birth date for Nathan Jr.'s oldest child, Rebecca Eliza, who was born in October of 1808. Given the calculated and known ages of his siblings, and the birth years of his children, it is all but certain that Nathan, Jr. was not born prior to 1775, but more likely later.

There was a deed recorded on June 7, 1776 in Southampton Deed Book 5, page 231, in which "Nathan Brett, Senr." bought a 75 acre tract from John Barrett. The fact that the deed called this Nathan "senior" indicates the existence of a Nathan, Jr. of age to be in the records, that being at least 21 years old. Nathan, Jr. who was the son of the Nathan who died in 1815, was too young to be the Nathan Jr. implied by this deed by twenty years. This means there were two (or more) Nathan, Jr.'s in the Southampton records.

On April 19, 1789, Nathan Brett, Sr. and Charity, his wife, sold "the last of my lands in Southampton" to Edward Brett. (Southampton Deed Book 7, page 222). The Nathan of the 1815 will listed his wife as Elizabeth. This basically proves the existence of two Nathan, Sr.'s in the Southampton records. Further analysis of the lands that the earlier Nathan, Sr. sold to Nathan, Jr. indicates they appear to be the same lands that the Nathan, Sr. in his 1815 will gave to his sons: Nathan, Jr., William G., Jesse, and John.

Note: It is believed that Charity, wife of Nathan Brett, Sr., is Charity Gatling. In her will, recorded in December of 1782, Sarah Gatling of Northampton County, North Carolina mentions her sister Charity Britt.

Conclusion: There are three Nathan Bretts in the records of Southampton County, Virginia. The first would have been born no later than 1751, and will be shown to have been born about 1715. The second would have been born no later than 1755, but was believed to have been born 1745-1750. The last Nathan would have been born after 1775. The first Nathan was known as either Nathan or Nathan, Sr. in the records. The second Nathan was listed as Nathan, Jr., then Nathan, and finally as Nathan, Sr. And the last was called in the Southampton records either Nathan, Jr. or Nathan after 1815.

Tax Lists

Old tax lists can be interesting. The tax lists for Southampton have survived from 1782 to the present. The lists do not tell who is kin to whom, but they can give some indications. In the tax list of 1782, there is both a Nathan and a Nathan, Jr. listed.

In the 1783 tax list, Nathan, Sr. is listed. Listed with him are Nathan, Jr. and Edward Brett. This is generally an indication that Nathan, Jr. and Edward, while of taxable age, were within Nathan Sr.'s household for whatever reason.

From 1784 through the 1786 tax lists, the three men (Nathan, Sr., Nathan, Jr., and Edward Brett) are listed separately but they follow each other in the tax lists as if they lived beside each other (and it is believed that this is the case).

The 1787 tax list is curious in that it lists both Nathan, Jr. and Edward, but also lists *"Nathan Brett, bell maker"*. Note: By her own admission to Joyce, Sue M. Brett never checked tax records in her quest to prove the family lore. She should have been thrilled when Joyce informed her of the bell maker tax reference.

Nathan, Jr. is listed in 1788 along with Nathan, Sr., but there are blank spaces beside Sr.'s name where the tax information would normally be. Generally this is seen when the tax payer has been exempted for reason of old age or infirmity. The tax list for 1789 is the same and is the last year the name Nathan, Sr. appears. In 1790, Nathan, Jr. is listed alone as Nathan, Jr. The implications are that Nathan, Sr. has passed away.

Daddy Nathan

No record has been found that says Nathan Brett and his wife Charity (Gatling) are the parents of the Nathan Brett who died in 1815 (who, bless his heart, left us a will). At this late date, some 200 years later, it is doubtful such a record will be found. Nevertheless, it is believed that Nathan and Charity were the parents of the Nathan who died in 1815.

Most of the lands that the elder Nathan obtained in Southampton eventually went to the younger Nathan. Some went to Edward Brett. At one time, the tax records show Nathan, Jr. to be in the household of Nathan, Sr. When not in the elder Nathan's household, Nathan, Jr. lived adjacent to him.

Nathan, Jr., who died 1815, named his second son William Gatling Brett, clearly an acknowledgment of his mother Charity Gatling Brett. Finally, all the known facts fit the family legend, even down to the elder Nathan being a bell maker. The odds of any of the legend being true are small. The odds of all of it being true, especially the part of Nathan being a bell maker, are phenomenal – unless the facts fit the legend and the legend is true. How often does one encounter bell makers in the records?

There were three successive generations of Nathan Brett in Southampton County, Virginia, from circa 1773 to circa 1825:

Nathan "The Bell Maker" Brett bc 1715-1789 and Charity Gatling, his wife.
Nathan Brett bc 1745 – 1815 and Elizabeth (Barrett?) his wife
Nathan Brett bc 1780 – dc 1825 and Mary N. Boone, his wife.

Origins of the Elder Nathan

A fragment of a page from an early Bertie County, North Carolina court minute book still survives. It is from 1738. In it is the request of Suzanna Bressie Brett to be the executrix of her husband's estate as per his will. Her husband was John Brett.

John Brett was probably born about 1660. In a 1690 deed in which he bought land in the upper parish of Isle of Wight County, Virginia, he is identified as a blacksmith (Isle of Wight Deed Book 1, page 27). John, the blacksmith, married Suzanna Bressie about 1695-97. They are both listed on a 1698 deed that shows John sold the land he bought in 1690 (Isle of Wight Deed Book 1, page 277). This was the start of a pattern for John and Suzanna – buying land, buying more land and selling the previous land, and all the while moving south. John, the blacksmith, and Suzanna, his wife, bought and sold land in the upper parish of Isle of Wight, the lower parish of Isle of Wight, and in that part of Isle of Wight that would become Southampton County in 1749. John was involved in no fewer than 7 Isle of Wight deeds.

By 1703, John is identified as living on the north bank of the Meherrin River in what was then known as Chowan Precinct, North Carolina (Isle of Wight Deed Book 2. page 329). By the time of his death on May 23, 1738, John had accumulated at least 1,700 acres of land by either deed or patent. At the time of his death, John lived in what was then Bertie County, North Carolina.

To date, a copy of John Brett's will has not been found. We know he made a will because his wife Suzanna was granted the administration of the will by Bertie Court and, in the ensuing years, there would be no fewer than 16 deeds referencing the will of John Brett as the origin of the property being sold. These deeds would be executed by four sons and one grandson of John, the blacksmith, Brett. These four sons have been identified as Thomas (probably the oldest as he bought land with John in 1719 – Chowan Precinct Deed dated February 12, 1710), Joseph, Benjamin, and Nathan. The grandson (also named John) inherited the last of the lands that John, the blacksmith, owned in Isle of Wight County, Virginia (Isle of Wight Deed Book 7, page 188).

Nathan Brett first enters the records of Bertie on January 23, 1739 when he witnessed a deed between his brothers Benjamin and Thomas. As a witness to a deed, Nathan had to have been at least 21. This would have put Nathan's birth year at or before 1717. Nathan's birth year has been estimated as 1715.

In 1741, Northampton County was formed from the western part of Bertie County. A large portion of the lands formerly belonging to John Brett would be in the new county.

Nathan is first positively identified as a son of John when, on 18 Nov 1751, Northampton Deed Book 1/502, he deeded 314 acres to Wm. Hart of Nansemond Co "devised 23 May 1738 by last will of FATHER, John Brett, Dec'd, of Bertie Co, NC.. The last we hear of Nathan being in Northampton County is on February 19, 1759 when he sold 60 acres of land (Northampton County Deed Book 2). When we next find Nathan, he is in Hertford County, North Carolina. Nathan did not move. In 1759 Hertford was formed from the eastern part of Northampton. Part of the John Brett lands that were acquired in Chowan became Bertie County lands, and then Northampton County lands would now be Hertford County lands. This included that part of the properties left to Nathan.

Other than a 1768 Hertford tax list that includes Nathan and his brother Thomas, Sr., nothing more is found of Nathan until he patented land on the Virginia side of the Virginia/North Carolina border in 1773. Unfortunately, the Hertford County Courthouse, along with the records it contained, burned – twice, once in the 1840's and again in 1862. The result is we have no way to know what other properties Nathan may have owned or when.

The move from the Meherrin River in Hertford County, North Carolina, to the part of Southampton County, Virginia, where Nathan patented land was not a large move. From Nathan's Southampton patent land to any point on the Meherrin in Hertford would have been from 4 to 10 miles. Even in Nathan's three mile per hour world, from his old property to his new would have been a two to five hour walk. And at some point during that walk, he would have had to pass by the Gatling plantation – the property of his in-laws. When the eldest Nathan sold that patent land to Edward Brett in April, 1789, he described the property as "the last of my lands in Southampton" rather than the last of my lands. This implies that Nathan did own or still owned land elsewhere, perhaps on the Meherrin in Hertford County, North Carolina.

As is often the case when researching families in the early 1700's, we have no one document that states that Nathan Brett, the bell maker, who patented land in Southampton in 1773 is the son of John Brett, the blacksmith, who died on the Meherrin in 1738 and Suzanna Bressie his wife. But the Nathan in Southampton is in- or close to- the right place at the right time to be the son of John the blacksmith. And with an absolute absence of any other records to suggest otherwise, it would seem that the Nathan in 1773 in Southampton is the son of John the blacksmith - whom it would seem would be the ideal and only teacher available to teach a young Nathan to make bells.

Author's note: Years and years ago, someone approached me because they needed help finding the ancestors of John H. G. Drake. Having gotten carried away with what I was doing, the information goes back as far as the information available, which makes it quite suitable for inclusion in this work.

The Ancestors of John Henry Gurley Drake

By Joe H. Drake

John H. G. Drake was born about 1839,[1] the son of John Gurley Drake[2] and Caroline Sumner.[3] [4] John and Caroline were married on July 15, 1833.[5] In addition to John Henry, other children of the family were:

Conrad (Council) born 1834,[6] died intestate April 12, 1873[7] [8]
Thadeous born 1838[9]
Emma born 1842[10]
Mary born 1844[11]
Samuel born 1848[12]

Caroline Sumner was the daughter of Byrd Sumner[13] [14] and his wife Nancy, maiden name as yet unknown. The farm upon which John and Caroline lived was 440 acres[15] in Nottoway Parish and had belonged to Caroline's father, Byrd. In March of 1840, Byrd transferred the property to the "Children of John Drake". The terms of the deed gave a life right to Byrd and Nancy his wife. The deed can be found in Southampton County Deed Book 24, page 470 and its wording is a bit strange reading in part:

"I Byrd Sumner, for and in consideration that John Drake ...will pay and discharge a judgement (sic) rendered against myself, the said John Drake and George Mountfort in the county court, court of Southampton at its March term 1820 in favor of Mills Sumner (which the said John Drake promises (sic) to do) hath given and granted... sell and confirm unto Conrad Byrd Sumner Drake, Thadeus Francis Williamson Drake, and John Henry Gurley Drake, children of said John and Caroline his wife" land where Byrd now resides, retaining (sic) life interest for him and his wife Nancy. Witness: Janes (sic) L. French, L.R. Edwards"

George Mountfort's connection with this deed is unknown, as is the witness James L. French. L. R. Edwards was clerk of the court at that time. Miles Sumner is believed to be Byrd Sumner's brother. Why Miles obtained a judgment against Byrd has not been researched.

---

[1] 1850 census, Southampton County, Virginia, page 325A.
[2] Ibid
[3] Ibid
[4] Southampton Marriage Bond Register, page 440
[5] Ibid
[6] 1850 census, Southampton County, Virginia, page 325A
[7] Southampton County Death Register
[8] Southampton County Court Order Book 1873-1881, ordered the estate of Conrad Drake committed to Sheriff William Briggs for administration by law, April 24, 1873.
[9] 1850 census, Southampton County, Virginia, page 325A
[10] Ibid
[11] Ibid
[12] Ibid
[13] Southampton Marriage Bond Register, page 440
[14] Southampton Deed Book 24, page 470
[15] Southampton Land Tax Books 1841 - 1850

In the 1850 census, the age of John Henry is given as 8 and the age of Emma as 10. This would have meant that John Henry was born in 1842. This is obviously incorrect as John Henry is named in the 1840 deed for the Byrd Sumner farm. The 1860 census lists John Henry as 21 and Emma as 18, which would seem to be more accurate than the 1850 census. Also listed in the John Gurley Drake household in 1850 are Mary and Anne Daughtry. Anne is Mary's daughter and Mary is sister to Caroline Sumner Drake. What Mary's husband's given name was and why she and her daughter Anne came to be living with John and Caroline has yet to be researched.

John Gurley Drake and his wife Caroline Sumner Drake both died intestate (i.e. without wills). John died on September 3, 1879[16]. Caroline died on April 15, 1872.[17] The disposition of the Byrd Sumner farm was has not been researched although, if Conrad was found to have no wife or children at his death, then his 1/3 of the property, by law, should have gone to John and Caroline and at their deaths to all of their remaining children. The other children of John and Caroline have yet to be researched.

John Gurley Drake was the son of Jeremiah Drake[18] and his wife Mary (Polly) Gurley[19]. Jeremiah was born about 1760 and Mary was born about 1765.

Mary Gurley was the daughter[20] of the Reverend George Gurley (1726 -1804) and his wife Mary Wills. The Reverend George Gurley was the pastor of St Luke's Episcopal parish both before (note that St. Luke's would have been the Church of England prior to the Revolution) and after the Revolution. One must use care when researching George Gurley as there were three: the oldest George[21] (1697-1771) came to Virginia from Scotland and was the father of the Rev. George of St. Luke's, the Rev. George[22] of St. Luke's also had a son George[23] who like his father was also a minister, and George III was a Methodist Minister who for many years was the pastor of Barnes Methodist Church.[24] The Reverend George of St. Luke's also had a son Joseph who followed his father as rector of St. Luke's parish.

Jeremiah and Mary were married October 8, 1787.[25] They were to have 8 children:

Jesse B.[26], born about 1789
Samuel B.[27], born about 1792
Nancy G.[28], born about 1794
Mary W.[29], born about 1799
John G.[30], born about 1801
Lucy F.[31], born about 1804
Elizabeth[32], born about 1806
Martha[33], born 1810

---

16 Southampton County Death Record
17 Ibid
18 Southampton County Order Book 1819-1822
Page 132, March 17, 1820
19 Ibid
20 Southampton County Wills, will of Rev. George (Jr.) Gurley
21 Ibid, will of George Gurley, Sr. recorded Jan.1, 1771
22 Southampton County Wills, will of Rev. George (Jr.) Gurley
23 Ibid
24 Historical Record of Barnes Methodist Church, by Betty W. Darden, private printing, 2002
25 Southampton County Marriage Bond Register, page 53
26 Southampton County Order Book 1819-1822
Page 132, March 17, 1820
27 Ibid
28 Ibid
29 Ibid
30 Ibid
31 Ibid
32 Ibid
33 Ibid

Jesse B. would marry Elizabeth Ridley Taylor on August 27, 1813.[34] Elizabeth was the daughter of Charles and Elizabeth Wood Taylor.[35] They were to have seven children: Elizabeth W., Margaret W., Mary G., Jeremiah Joseph, Samuel, Lucretia, and John.[36] Jesse B. died in September of 1825.[37]

Samuel B. seems to have died about 1836[38] leaving no record as having ever been married.

Nancy G. married Zachariah Blythe on October 24, 1824[39] No other genealogical records have been found on Nancy and Zachariah.

Mary W. – No marriage or death records have been found to date but as Mary was not mentioned in her mother's will,[40] it is believed she died prior to 1837.

John G. – see previous pages 1 and 2

Lucy F. married Carr Wiggins on October 10, 1828[41] No records in regards to Lucy's children or death date have been located.

Elizabeth married James Brock on December 31, 1828.[42] Elizabeth died without issue in 1832.[43]

Martha was never married and died in 1839.[44]

Jeremiah and Mary lived on what was supposed to be a 500 acre[45] farm that ran along the west side of the Nottoway River in St. Luke's parish at what was the small village of Monroe. Today Monroe Road runs through the northern part of the farm. When the farm was surveyed in 1825, it actually measured 736 acres[46] total. Jeremiah had inherited the land from his father Jesse by right of primogenitor.

Jeremiah died in 1811 leaving a nuncupative will which "loaned" all the estate - both real and personal - to his wife, Mary, during her life or widowhood. Afterwards the real estate was to be divided between his sons and the personal property was to be divided among all his children.[47] This seemingly simple will would create problems and an estate that would last for more than 25 years[48] before finally being closed.

The problem was that, while Jeremiah had loaned Mary everything, he left her nothing. Mary was a widow, perhaps in her late thirties, with eight children at home. Only one of those eight was grown or of legal age. She had to maintain a plantation which did not belong to her (it belonged to her sons). If there was a bad crop year, Mary

---

34 Southampton County Marriage Bond Register, page 661
35 Ridley of Southampton by Lyndon Hart & Bromfield Nichol, page 445.
36 Ibid
37 Southampton County Court Records, Order Book 1838-1839, pg 518
38 Southampton County, Virginia, Court Records, Order Book 1835-1839, Feb. 18, 1839 Fielding J. Mahone appointed administrator of the estate.
39 Southampton County Marriage Bond Register, page 450
40 Southampton County Wills, WB 12, pg 90.
41 Southampton County Marriage Bond Register, page 355
42 Southampton County Marriage Bond Register, page 393
43 Southampton County Land Tax Books 1782-1849.
44 Southampton Deed Book 24, page 462
45 Southampton County Land Tax Books, 1782-1849
46 Southampton County Platt Book 1
47 Southampton County Will Book 7, page 89
48 Southampton County Order Book 1835-1839, pg 200, Nov. 21, 1836
Ordered the estate of Jeremiah Drake to be committed to the hands of Benjamin Griffin, Shrf. for administration by law.

could not sell any of the 13[49] slaves to make ends meet – they did not belong to her. Like everything else, they were only loaned to her. This was also true of the horses or cows. Nor could Mary borrow any money to use to plant crops. She had no collateral.

Mary's solution to this problem was to have her children sue her to break the will. A nuncupative will such as Jeremiah's is an oral will generally given on a one's deathbed in the presence of witnesses. Under the law at that time, nuncupative wills could not be used to transfer real estate. Jeremiah's will was thus broken and the estate divided as if he had died intestate.

The Chancery Order Book recorded the outcome (all spelling as original):

Southampton County Order Book 1819-1822
Page 132, March 17, 1820

In Chancery

Samuel Drake, Jesse Drake, Nancy G. Drake and Mary W., John, Lucy T.,
Eliza, and Martha Drake infants by Samuel Drake their (???) friend. Plffs.

against

Mary Drake widow of Jeremiah Drake decs. Defendants

This day this cause came on to be heard on the writt, answer and exhibits, when it was ordered adjudged and decreed by the court, that Clements Rochelle, William E. Daughtry, James Bishop, and John Rochelle or any three be commissioners to divide the slaves belonging to the estate of Jeremiah Drake dec. (except a negro man Brister) in eight equal parts and asign one eighth part to each of the complaintants (???) Jesse B. Drake, Samuel Drake, Nancy G. Drake, Mary W. Drake, John Drake, Lucy Drake, Eliza Drake, and Martha Drake and the same commission, after allotting to Mary Drake, widow of the said Jeremiah Drake decs.one third part of the stock, household and kitchen furniture and plantation utensils, proceed to sell the other two thirds fo the stock, household and kitchen furniture to the highest bidder upon a credit of six months and asigning one eighth parts to each of the complaintants Jesse B. Drake, Samuel Drake, Mary W. Drake, Nancy G. Drake, John Drake, Lucy T. Drake, Eliza Drake, and Martha Drake and that they report to this court in order to afinal decree.

Division of the lands of Jeremiah - 736 acres - surveyed July 13, 1825
Plot 1- 63 acres
Plot 2- 63 acres
Plot 3- 65 acres
Plot 4- 100 acres
Plot 5- 90 acres
Plot 6- 94 acres
Plot 7- 64 acres
Plot 8- 20 acres
Dower land - 20 acres and 157 acres

Note the reference to "a negro man Brister". His name was actually Brisco. When Jeremiah's grandfather, John Drake, made his will[50] on September 14, 1767, he directed that his slave "Brisco "serve 15 years until my younger children are grown and then be granted his freedom". After John's death in 1770, Brisco fulfilled his duties to John's second wife Winnefred, gained his freedom, and continued to live on the plantation working for Jeremiah's

[49] Southampton County Personal Property Tax List for 1811
[50] Southampton County Will Book 2, page 361

father, Jesse, and then Jeremiah and Jeremiah's widow. At the time of the suit, he had been with the family for more than 53 years.

The death of Jesse B. in 1825,[51] followed by the death of Elizabeth in 1830,[52] Samuel in 1836,[53] Mary Gurley in 1837,[54] and both Martha[55] and Mary W.[56] in 1839 initiated a series of no less than 5 Chancery cases involving the estate of Jeremiah and how the land and negroes should be divided.[57] From 1818 to 1840, there were no less than 25 deeds and deeds of trusts and/or releases executed on the lands of Jeremiah. Jesse B. sold 20 acres[58] to Jacob Barnes to be surveyed at some point in the future as well as signing two deeds of trust[59] on lands which he was yet to possess. At least one of those deeds of trust was in default at the death of Jesse B.[60] The bulk of the lands of Jeremiah were bought by Edwin Beale and his son John. Fielding Mahone, who was Martha's guardian, bought her portion at her death[61] and built a brick house upon it, part of which stands today. Supposedly it was in this house that Fielding's son, CSA Maj. Gen. William Mahone was born.

John G. Drake sold the last of the lands of Jeremiah to John Beale in 1840.[62] This was the same year he gained the lands of his father-in-law Byrd Sumner and paid Byrd's judgment to Miles Sumner.

Jeremiah Drake was the son[63] of Jesse Drake and his wife Ann. Despite extensive research, the maiden name of Ann is as yet unknown. Ann may have been an Ellis as there is some circumstantial evidence to indicate such.

Jesse is believed to have been born about 1720 as he was the only grandchild in the 1739 will of his grandfather, Dr. Samuel Browne, to not have his legacy restricted by the term "when of age 21", indicating that Jesse was nearly that age at that time. His wife, Ann, may have been 18 to 20 years younger than Jesse. Ann was born about 1738 and she died intestate in 1793.

Although Jesse left a will,[64] he did not mention his children individually. Because of their many associations with Ann after the death of Jesse, the children of Jesse and Ann are believed to be:

Jeremiah, born about 1760
Drewry, born about 1763
Elizabeth, born about 1768
Dorothy, born about 1770
Mary (Polly), born about 1771.

Jesse made his will on November 25, 1768, and it was recorded on May 13, 1773. It is a short will that leaves all the "movables" to his wife during her life or widowhood, after which the estate is to be divided among "all my children". No real estate is mentioned in the will although Jesse owned a 300 acre tract that was willed to him by his

---

[51] Southampton County, Virginia, Court Records, Order Book 1838-1839, pg 518, Feb. 18, 1839, John M. Gurley appointed administrator of Jesse's estate.
[52] Southampton County Land Tax Books 1782-1849.
[53] Southampton County, Virginia, Court Records, Order Book 1835-1839, Feb. 18, 1839, Fielding J. Mahone appointed administrator of the estate.
[54] Southampton County, Virginia, Court Records, Order Book 1835-1839, Feb. 18, 1839, Fielding J. Mahone appointed administrator of the estate.
[55] Southampton County Deeds, DB 24, pg 462.
[56] Ibid
[57] Southampton County Chancery Cases 1820-005, 1826-003, 1837-013, 1838-013, and 1839-010
[58] Southampton County Deed Book 16, page 223
[59] Southampton County Deed Book 16, page 325, Deed Book 17, page 341
[60] Southampton County Deed Book 20, page 138
[61] Southampton County Deed Book 24, page 459
[62] Southampton County Deed Book 24, page 514
[63] Southampton County Land Tax Books 1782-1849
[64] Southampton County Will Book 3, page 51

grandfather, Dr. Samuel Browne, and at the death of his father, John, he would gain possession of the 500 acre tract that Dr. Browne had left to Jesse's mother, Mary.[65] Jesse avoided using the word "loan" in his will which would cause Mary Gurley so much trouble at the death of Jeremiah.

Because Jesse had made no provisions in his will for the distribution of his lands, and because he died before the United States gained its independence, English inheritance laws governed what was to become of his real estate. This meant that as the oldest son (the right of primogenitor), all the real estate went to Jeremiah, less a one-third life estate as a dower to his mother Ann.

Drewry was born about 1763.[66] At the death of Ann he seems to gain one of the dower slaves.[67] The 1810 census indicates that he was living on or very near Jeremiah's land, perhaps farming the land that had been the dower of Ann. From the tax lists, it appears that Jeremiah and Drewry had a very close working relationship in that, whenever Jeremiah would lose a horse or slave on the tax list, Drewry would gain a horse or slave and vice versa.[68] After the death of Jeremiah, Drewry appears to have moved to the lands of Thomas Barnes, his brother-in-law who married his sister Dorothy. Drewry married Sarah Kitchen, daughter of William and Martha Kitchen on April 14, 1792.[69] The children of Drewry and Sarah are believed to be Thomas, Drewry, Jr., Hines, Martha, Sarah, Jeremiah, William, and Nancy.

Elizabeth married William Bradley on February 2, 1790.[70] Jeremiah provided the bond.[71] The 1791 tax list shows Ann with two taxable males over 16. These are believed to be Drewry and William Bradley.

Dorothy was born about 1770. Dorothy married Thomas Barnes on March 4, 1807[72] whom she had sued for child support in March of 1804.[73] The case was continued and eventually dropped when Thomas and Dorothy were wed. Dorothy died about 1832. Her union with Thomas would produce one child, a girl also named Dorothy. Dorothy's brother-in-law was the Jacob Barnes who would buy 20 acres from Jesse B. Drake (son of Jeremiah) without knowing exactly what 20 acres he was buying.

Mary (Polly) was born about 1771. She wed Newit Edwards on October 20, 1800. The Edwards plantation was no more than 2 miles from the lands of Jesse. The bond was provided by George Gurley (Jeremiah's father-in-law).

In the will of Dr. Samuel Browne, Jesse's grandfather,[74] he inherited in 1740 a 300 acre farm adjoining and just to the north of the 500 acres that Dr. Browne would leave his daughter, Mary Browne Drake. Under English common law, Mary as a married woman could not own land in her own right. She had to share ownership with her husband, John Drake. When Mary Browne Drake died intestate about 1748, Jesse, as the oldest son inherited the 500 acres. But Jesse could not take possession of the land for John "by right of his wife" held a life estate to the property. John would remarry a woman no older, if as old, as Jesse. When John died in 1770, not only would Jesse gain possession of the 500 acre home plantation, but also 8 more mouths to feed: his stepmother and 7 half-brothers and half-sisters ranging in age from about 7 to 18 years old.

In January of 1773, Jesse sold the 300 acre tract from his grandfather to his cousin Dr. Sam Browne II.[75] In April his stepmother recorded the deed to a small 67 acre farm no more than 3 miles from Jesse's 500 acre tract.[76] Soon thereafter, perhaps in May, Jesse died.[77]

---

65 Ibid
66 1810 census for Southampton County
67 Southampton County Tax Lists 1782 - 1850
68 Ibid
69 Southampton Marriage Bond Register, page 82
70 Ibid, page 64
71 Ibid
72 Southampton County Marriage Bond Register, page 170
73 Southampton County Court Minute Book , 1804
74 Isle of Wight County Will Book 4, page 274
75 Southampton County Deed Book 4, page 547

The parents of Jesse were John Drake and Mary Browne. Mary was the oldest child of Dr. Browne's second marriage to Mary Jones. She was born about 1702 and was probably still in her late teens when she married John Drake and bore Jesse. Mary died intestate about 1748. Dr. Browne's first wife is unknown, but she bore him four sons. Note that Jeremiah died at about age 50, as did Jesse. Mary was only about 46 when she passed away. None of Dr. Browne's first four sons lived to the age of 40. Of Jeremiah's children, Jesse B. died at age 37 or so, Samuel at about 36, and Mary W., Martha, and Elizabeth all died before the age of 30. Dr. Charles E. Drake, a member of the family and a cardiologist, speculates that the family may have had a genetic predisposition to heart disease or a genetic weakness in the heart muscle.[78]

Between the years 1715 and 1731, Dr. Browne patented more than 2,000 acres on the west side of the Nottoway River (St. Luke's parish).[79] It was on part of this land that he moved his daughter and her new husband, probably about 1720. John and his family would be the first Drakes and only Drakes on the west side of the river for 100 years. This would be the same land that Dr. Browne would leave to Mary and Jesse in his will. Dr. Browne made his home on the east side of the Nottoway River in Nottoway Parish.

John Drake was born about 1695.[80] His first wife was Mary Browne whom he wed about 1719. John and Mary were to have seven children.[81] John referred to these as "my older children" in his will.[82]

Jesse, born about 1720
Samuel Nicholas, born about 1725
Mary, born about 1727
Martha, born about 1721
Thomas, born about 1733
Penelope, born about 1735
John, born about 1737

Jesse has been discussed above.

Samuel Nicholas seems to have died soon after Dr. Browne's will was recorded.

Mary would marry Robert Grimmer. They relocated to Pitt County, NC, prior to December, 1762, where Robert witnessed a deed when his brother-in-law, John, bought land in Pitt.[83]

Martha married William Battle. It is believed they lived on a plantation just to the south of Smith Ferry on the Nottoway River. Smith Ferry was where US 258 crosses the Nottoway River today. Up until the mid-1970's, this area was know as "Battle's Beach". Martha and William were known to have children Ann, Charity, Isaac, and Joel.[84]

Thomas moved to Pitt County, NC, prior to 1763. In that year he married Elizabeth Atkinson, daughter of Amos Atkinson. Thomas bought from his brother John the land in Pitt County that John had bought in 1762.[85] Thomas died in Pitt County about 1795. He was father to four daughters: Elizabeth, Mary, Martha, and Lucrecy.[86]

---

76 Southampton County Deed Book 4, page 529
77 Southampton County Will Book 3, page 51
78 Conversations with the author
79 "They Crossed the Blackwater", Pete Joyner, Appendix C
80 John Drake signed a petition in 1722 to have the Colonial government place a customs house on the Blackwater or Nottoway. He would have been 21 or more at that time.
81 Southampton County Will Book 2, page 361
82 Ibid
83 Pitt County, NC, Deed Book B, page 376
84 DRAKE, Paul: Now in Our Fourth Century: Copyright 1999, page 519
85 Pitt County, NC Deed Book C, page 475
86 DRAKE, Charles E., genealogical notes and emails.

Penelope married Joseph Barrow.[87] This couple has yet to be researched.

John bought and sold land in Pitt County, NC, bought land in Southampton in 1769, and sold the land in 1779. He shows up in the Land Tax book as owning 100 acres in 1792 and keeps this land for nearly 20 years without the benefit of a recorded deed. That is all that has been learned of John to date. It is doubtful that John lived in Southampton for, while he paid real estate taxes, he was never listed on the personal property tax lists. John remains a mystery.

John's second wife was Winnefred whose maiden name has not been found. She was born about 1723 and married John around 1751. Winnefred's will was recorded on January 19, 1801. John and Winnefred were to have seven children:[88]

Molly, born about 1759. She married an unknown Woddill.[89]
Honor, born about 1757. She married an unknown Pope.[90]
Zillar, born about 1755. She also married an unknown Pope.[91]
Isaac, born about 1761. As he was not mentioned in his mother's will,[92]
Isaac is believed to have died prior to 1800.
Jonas, born about 1752
Jordan, born about 1763
Joel, born about 1755

Jonas moved to the Halifax district of Martin county, NC, prior to 1790 as he was listed on that census. He later shows up on the 1787 Nash County, NC, tax lists. His wife, Charity (maiden name unknown) reported his estate inventory in Nash County in 1815. Jonas is known to have had one daughter, Martha.[93]

Jordan bought three tracts of land in Northampton County, NC, from 1789 to 1802.[94] He sold this land in 1803 and 1807[95] and moved to Warren County, Ohio, with his brother Joel. Jordan was married to Martha (last name unknown). Jordan died April 29, 1837. Jordan and Martha had 10 children.[96]

Like his brother Jordan, Joel also bought three tracts of land in Northampton from 1795 to 1804[97] and sold them in 1807[98] to move to Warren County, Ohio, with Jordan. Joel was a Methodist Minister who founded Olive Grove Methodist Church in Warren County. Joel was twice married. His first marriage was to Rebecah Ward of Northampton County. After Rebecah's death, Joel married Sally (LNU). Joel was a veteran of the Revolution and witnessed the surrender of Cornwallis at Yorktown. Joel left a will in Warren County, Ohio, when he died in 1840 in which he names four children.

---

87 Ibid.
88 Southampton County Will Book 2, page 361
89 Southampton County Will Book 5, page 245
90 Ibid
91 Ibid
92 Ibid
93 Barbara Marshall genealogical notes found in the archives of the "Drake-L" message board.
94 Northampton County Deeds 8-92, 10-124, 12-55
95 Ibid, 12-119, 13-109
96 WARREN CO OHIO PROBATE COURT OCP BX73 #22
97 Northampton County Deeds, 8-93, 12-383, 12-492

98 Ibid, 13-274, 13-391, 13-302

The parents of John Drake[99] were Thomas (TD) Drake and Ann Griffin[100]. Ann was born about 1678 to Owen Griffin and Mary Hunt Edwards (widow of Robert Edwards)[101]. Ann died before 1778.[102] John and Ann were married about 1694.

Thomas was born about 1675.[103] He is known to researchers as TD because that is the mark he used to sign his legal documents. Thomas was probably born in that part of Isle of Wight County that is on the east side of the Blackwater River opposite Joyner's Bridge. In 1713 Thomas patented two parcels of land in that part of Isle of Wight that was to be formed into Southampton in 1749.[104] He patented two other parcels in 1723[105] and one in 1731,[106] 1060 acres total. The land was centered around what is today the intersection of Story Station Road and Bethel Road, just to the north of old Nottoway Chapel between Courtland and Sedley. TD sold two of the parcels before he died in 1758. He left one parcel to his son William and the remaining two he left to son Thomas. This did not seem to bother the oldest son John who had more than enough of his wife's land. The youngest son, Lazarus, sued William and Thomas in 1759 over the will but did not win.[107]

Thomas's will was recorded on May 11, 1758.[108] In the will he names his children:

John, born about 1695
William, born about 1697
Thomas, born about 1699
Mary, born about 1710
Lazarus, born about 1712

John has been discussed.

William married Mary (last name unknown) and lived to be a very old man, passing away in 1784.[109] William and Mary were childless.

Thomas inherited the homeplace and cared for his mother until her death. He married Sarah (last name unknown) and had two children: Mary and Celia. Mary never married. Celia married Absolum Joyner on June 8, 1781.[110] Thomas left his farm to wife Sarah and daughter Mary as a life estate and then the farm was to go to his grandson Joseph Joyner.[111]

Mary married William Williams and had seven children: Simon, Benjamin, Elisha, Michael, Elizabeth, Mary, and Penelope.[112]

Lazarus moved to Sussex County and married Sarah Hines. He later moved to Edgecombe County, NC, where he died on February 20, 1783. The children of Lazarus and Sarah are: Elizabeth, Jesse, William, David, Sally, Ann, Hines, and Drury.[113]

---

99 Southampton County Will Book 1, page 254
100 Isle of Wight Wills, Chapman, Page 115.
101 DRAKE, Paul: Now in Our Fourth Century: Copyright 1999.
102 A deed of Hardy Johnson in 1778 mentions line formerly of Ann Drake, decd. Southampton Cty. DB 5, pp 135-136.
103 DRAKE, Charles E., genealogical notes and emails.
104 Land Patent Book 10, pages 99 and 120
105 Ibid, Book 11, pages 254, 255
106 Ibid, Book 14, page 284
107 Southampton Order Book 1759-1763, pg. 18
108 Southampton County Will Book 1, page 254
109 Southampton County Land Tax Books 1782-1849.
110 Southampton County Marriage Bond Register
111 Southampton County Will Book 4, page 95
112 DRAKE, Paul: Now in Our Fourth Century: Copyright 1999
113 Ibid

Thomas (TD) was the son of John Drake[114] and Jemima Parnell. Jemima was the daughter of Richard Parnell. She was born about 1652 and died some time after 1694 when she gave a sworn deposition to the Isle of Wight Court.[115]

John was born in 1646 in South Petherton Parish, Somerset, England.[116] He came to Jamestown in 1658 with his family as an indentured servant with 10 years to serve.[117] If his head right and indenture were not sold (it is very possible it was), John spent his adolescence at Smith's Fort Plantation in Surry County.[118] John Drake's name appears on a transcription of a 1677 petition to King Charles II, asking for a pardon of Isle of Wight men for their part in Bacon's Rebellion.[119]

In 1682, John patented 100 acres close to Joyner's Bridge on the east side of the river.[120] This patent was never perfected and thus lost probably due to the death of John.[121]

The children of John and Jemima are:[122]

John, born about 1673
Thomas (TD), born about 1675
Richard (R), born about 1677

John was married, but the name of his wife is not known. There is some learned speculation that she may have been a Scott or Exum. John patented land a bit to the east of the lands of Thomas (TD).[123] John's will was recorded on July 12, 1752,[124] and it gives the names of his children: Mary, Ann, Timothy, Ester, Joshua, Thomas and Barnaby.

Thomas (TD) has been discussed.

Richard (R) like his brother, Thomas, is known to researchers by the mark he used to sign documents – R. Richard married Sarah (last name unknown) by whom he had only one child, a daughter named for her mother. Richard patented land between Thomas (TD) and Nottoway Chapel and adjoining both.[125] Richard died before 1762.[126]

John was the son of Richard Drake and his wife Thomazine.[127] Richard was probably born about 1615 most likely in either Somerset or Devon, England. Richard was a serge maker by trade (weaver of a certain type of woolen

---

[114] National Genealogic Society Quarterly-Origins of the Drake Family of Isle of Wight County, Virginia – Vol. 79 (1001 by Charles E. Drake.

[115] Ibid

[116] Baptismal Register, South Petherton Parish, Somerset, England, located and recorded by Charles E. Drake, baptized on May 3, 1647, thus was probably born in 1646. To author by email from CED.

[117] National Genealogic Society Quarterly-Origins of the Drake Family of Isle of Wight County, Virginia - Charles E. Drake.

[118] Paul Drake via email to author.

[119] Isle of Wight court records, original has not been examined.

[120] Patent Book 7, page 182

[121] National Genealogic Society Quarterly-Origins of the Drake Family of Isle of Wight County, Virginia – Vol. 79 (1991) by Charles E. Drake.

[122] Ibid

[123] Virginia Land Patents, Book 11: 445, Library of Virginia

[124] Southampton County Will Book 1, page 124

[125] Patent Book 10, pages 102 and 108

[126] National Genealogic Society Quarterly-Origins of the Drake Family of Isle of Wight County, Virginia - Charles E. Drake.

[127] Ibid

cloth). In 1658 he indentured his entire family to gain passage to Virginia.[128] What happened to Richard and Thomazine or their daughter Mary after their arrival at Jamestown is unknown.

The children of Richard and Thomazine are:

Mary, born about 1642. No information has been found on her after leaving Bristol, England.

John has been discussed.

Thomas was born in April 1, 1659, and like his brother John was baptized at the church at South Petherton Parish, Somerset.[129] Thomas bought land on the Meherrin River in that part of Chowan County, NC, that would become Hertford County. This land was sold by his oldest son, Aaron, in 1727 indicating that Thomas died prior to that date. Thomas's wife is unknown. His children are believed to be Aaron, Richard, Arnold, John, and Thomas.[130] Richard stayed in Southampton while the other children of Thomas moved to various parts of North Carolina. Richard is known in the records of the County as Richard, Jr. to distinguish him from his older cousin Richard (R),

---

[128] Bristol, England data base of emigrants to the new world. Available on line at the Virtual Jamestown website.

[129] Baptismal Register, South Petherton Parish, Somerset, England, located and recorded by Charles E. Drake, To author by email from CED.

[130] National Genealogic Society Quarterly-Origins of the Drake Family of Isle of Wight County, Virginia - Charles E. Drake.

Family Shorts

Short tales and blurbs not to be confused with underwear or pants from Bermuda

A MATTER OF PRIDE

William Henry Harrison Chitty, the author's great-great-grandfather was a veteran of the 32cd North Carolina Infantry. The 32cd left garrison duty in various places in 1863 to become part of the 2cd Corps, Army of Northern Virginia in time for the Gettysburg campaign. The regiment remained with the Army of Northern Virginia until its surrender at Appomattox on April 9, 1865. William, however, was wounded and was captured by the Union forces in a hospital in Richmond on April 2cd.

We don't know a lot about William as a person. From the lone story we do have, you would have to draw the conclusion he had a lot of pride or vanity. My great-grandfather, William's son-in-law, Joseph Franklin Cowan, told the tale of how one day William, his sons, hired man, and son-in-law were working together on some chore on the farm when a salesman came by. The salesman looked them over and asked if he might speak to the man in authority. Great-great-grandfather seemed upset that the man was unable to identify his exalted status as the leader the clan and man-in-charge of the farming operation. From that day forward, until the day he died, William Henry Harrison Chitty would only wear white shirts with a tie.

THE BLIND MULE

According to my Granddaddy Rufus, he had a blind mule that ate every frog he saw. To a young boy of six or seven, this was a shocking revelation: "the mule ate frogs??!!!" Yeah, he got me. He smiled as he walked away. Eventually the boy figured it out.

PAVLOV'S DOG

Ivan Pavlov wasted his time. He observed dogs salivating at sight of red meat and used that revelation to train the dogs to react to a bell. He became famous as a physiologist when he published the results of his tests in 1897. He called it conditioned reflexes. Ivan Pavlov could have gotten the same information by visiting any farm.

Granddaddy Rufus always had cows. Back in the 1920's and 1930's, he had 8 to 12 head of Guernsey and/or Jersey cows. Twice a day, at about the same time each morning and at about the same time each late afternoon, the cows would come up to the little milking shed. He did not have to call them; the cows knew the time. There at the shed Granddaddy Rufus would feed them a bit of corn from a tin bucket and he hand-milked each one. He separated the cream from the milk and fed the milk to the hogs. The cream he carried to Franklin to be made into ice cream.

Ok, city folks and young'uns, it is country education time again. What comes to mind when someone thinks of milk cows is those huge white and black beasts called Holsteins. Holsteins are the most popular commercial breed of milk cows by far because they are heavy milkers. During the 300 days a year the cows are milked, it is not unusual for a Holstein to give 25,000 pounds of milk, or nearly 10 gallons per day. The brown and white Guernsey and Jersey cows are much smaller breeds and give far less milk but the butter fat content of their milk is much higher than the Holstein, giving those breeds the edge when producing cream.

Granddaddy Rufus loved cows. Even after he gave up the milk cows, until he was 80 or more, he would always keep 15 to 25 feeder calve steers to be fattened out and sold. He preferred the red with a white face Hertford beef cows to the black with a white face Angus beef cows. He would buy the calves when they weighed 400 to 600 pounds and feed them until they weighed 1,500 to 2,000 pounds. Every morning and every evening Granddaddy would hand-feed grain to the cows, making sure he rattled his tin bucket in the process. During the day they ate grass in the pasture.

It was during a particularly dry summer, in which the Great Cypress Swamp could be crossed in several places, that the calves got out of the pasture. They wound up a bit over a mile and half on the other side of the swamp from the barn in which Granddaddy fed them. There aren't many roads that cross the swamp. To get from our farm to the opposite side of the swamp by vehicle is a trip of a bit over 7 miles. Granddaddy wasn't worried. He fixed the hole in the fence, grabbed his tin bucket, said "let's go", and around to the other side of the swamp we went.

When we got to the other side, there were the calves - in a corn field, munching on the leaves of a neighbor's crop. Granddaddy Rufus walked across the field to the edge of the woods, called to the calves, rattled the tin bucket, and disappeared into the woods with a line of calves dutifully following behind. The Pied Piper of Hamlin would have been envious of Granddaddy. After we watched him disappear, we took a minute or two to confer with the neighbor as to damages (he good-naturedly said there was none). We got back in the pickup and retraced our journey of 7 miles back around the swamp to the farm. When we got there, Granddaddy was closing the gate of the pasture.

Ivan Pavlov, his dog, and his bell got nothing on Granddaddy Rufus with his tin bucket.

THE BANANA

All my life I have been rather large. But I have been blessed in that I do not have to worry about being fat – my family takes care of that for me. Always have even from a young age.

Daddy R. E. always loved to tell this tale. For some reason or another, we were all at the home of my great-grandfather, Joseph Franklin Cowan. And when I say all the family, we are referring to 2 great aunts, my grandmother, 4 uncles and their wives, an aunt and her husband, my parents, my brothers and 9 cousins – a total of 28 people (and one sister and cousin had yet to be born). On the front porch in a high back rocking chair sat the old man, my great-grandfather. In his hand was the biggest, yellowiest, sweetest ripe banana there ever was. Beside his chair stood a chubby but really cute boy of 4 – me.

Joseph Franklin Cowan, my namesake, looked at me and then looked at the banana. And he said to me: "I know it looks good, but you can't have any." How thoughtful, even in the last year of his long life at the age of 90, he showed empathy for the physical well-being and plight of his slightly overweight great-grandson – mean old man.

THE TURKEY HUNT

Thomas Harrison Drake spent four years, April 17, 1861 to April 26, 1865, with the 17th North Carolina Infantry in the Confederate Army. We don't know for certain but one would suppose he spent many, if not most, of those nights sleeping on the ground or if lucky in a tent. Even for a man in his early twenties, this type of lifestyle had to take its toll on his body. In his later years Thomas developed arthritis in his knees and hips to the extent that he could only walk short distances at the time, and then only with the aid of either one or two canes.

But he still loved to hunt. He had what appeared to be a 12 gauge double-barrel muzzle-loading shotgun. Even after the advent of breach-loading shotguns that used shells, Thomas kept using his old muzzle-loader shotgun. I have often wondered if that preference for the old muzzle-loader might have been tied to his war years when all he had was a muzzle-loading rifle and his life depended on it. I haven't seen that old shotgun in years as my older brother has it. It was well-worn as I recall. There was also a powder horn. What was really cool was that Thomas had taken a stick, about an inch and a quarter in diameter and around three inches long, and had hollowed out or cupped each end of this short stick - like an hour glass plugged in the middle and open on the ends. One end of the cupped stick held just the right amount of gun powder to load the shotgun; the other end held just the right amount of shot. Wish I knew what became of it. I have yet to see anything else like it anywhere.

When Thomas first found he had to give up walking to hunt, he would have one of his sons hitch a mule to the cart and haul him to one likely place or another. Later when he figured the turkeys were seeing him before he saw them, he had his boys build him a turkey blind to hide in. Of course there was still no guarantee that Tom and the turkeys were both going to be in the same place at the right time so Thomas decided to tip the scales in his favor. He started leaving a small pile of corn in front of his blind. I do not know if it was illegal then, but today baiting wildlife is very, very illegal – the kind of illegal that gets your guns seized, the kind of illegal that gets your truck impounded, the kind of illegal that comes with large fines and your hunting license revoked. The good news is that, after more than 120 years, I'm fairly certain the statute of limitations has run out for Thomas.

Early one day Thomas had the boys hitched the mule to the cart and hauled him to his blind. He had the boys put out a little pile of corn and told the boys to come fetch him at sunset. They said they would get him at lunch. No he was fine – he had a couple of baked sweet potatoes in his pocket. So as the boys left, there sat the antique man –

with his antique gun, behind his blind looking at the little pile of corn, a walking cane leaning against his arthritic knee.

Toward sunset Thomas's sons went to fetch him from his blind. They heard him whistling from a hundred yards away. They rounded the bend in the path and there was Thomas just as happy as he could be. In front of the blind, at the little pile of corn, were five dead turkeys - each shot through the head with a single shot from the old muzzle-loader shotgun.

UNCLE LEWIS'S HORSE

Granddaddy Rufus had an older half-brother. Uncle Lewis was born 1867, making him 22 years older than Granddaddy and 33 years older than his youngest brother Allen. Lewis was an entrepreneur. In the little town of Newsoms he owned the hardware store and a general store. At some point Lewis and a cousin founded the Newsoms Telephone Company.

Always looking for another chance to make another dollar or two, when the United States post office was looking for someone to carry the mail between Newsoms, Virginia, and Lotta, North Carolina (while stopping at Sands, Virginia, along the way, a distance of about 10 miles), Lewis got the job. The train would throw out a sack of mail as it sped by on the way to Franklin if east-bound or to Boykins if west-bound. The post office would sort the mail for Sands and Lotta. Lewis would hitch his horse to his buggy and start his rounds.

If you look for Lotta on the map, you won't find it. It no longer exists. It was located about 2 miles south of the Virginia/North Carolina state line on what is today called Statesville Road. And when it did exist, there wasn't a great deal to it: a two story country store with one corner dedicated for the post office. The storekeeper/postmaster lived on the second floor with his family. Nothing remains of that building today except a clump of trees which took over the site as the building succumbed to time and termites.

On the other hand, Sands is still there. It no longer has a post office. The hamlet originally was known as Piney Woods and was forced to change its name to Sands when post office found it already had another Piney Woods. Sands boasted 3 houses, a little barber shop, a big barn and a country store/post office. One of the houses and the store building still remain.

Most of Lewis's kin thought he had a problem with alcohol. Lewis didn't think so. He would get his quart of moonshine, get drunk, pass out – no problem. Lewis would get the outgoing Newsoms mail, get in the buggy and be off, usually with a bottle of liquor. His first stop was Sands to drop off the incoming mail. His next was in Lotta where he dropped off the incoming and picked up the outgoing mail. By this time Lewis was good and drunk. Generally, somewhere between Lotta and Sands on the return, Lewis would pass out.

At this point, the horse was not only the mode of power but also the designated driver of the enterprise. The horse had covered the route so many times it was second nature to him. The horse walked to Sands for the second time and stopped. Someone would come out the store/post office, retrieve the mail, and put in the outgoing mail being careful not to disturb the sleeping Lewis. They would give the horse a sugar cube, tap his rump, and off he walked to the Newsoms Post Office.

Uncle Lewis needed that horse. The horse did not really need Lewis. For the price of a couple sugar cubes, the horse could have done the job by himself.

STRONG IN BODY

Little smart-ass chubby 6 year old to Granddaddy Rufus: "Granddaddy, are you strong?"

Granddaddy Rufus stood a little bit taller, his head was held a bit higher. This was a chance to look good to one of his grandsons: "Yeah, I guess I am fairly strong."

"I thought I smelled you!" Uncontrollable laughter from the 6 year old at his own joke.

From that day forward, whenever we first encountered during the day, Granddaddy Rufus made it a point to tell me he was "strong in body, and sweet in smell."

A FARMER'S WORK

This little piece is not about family. It is not humorous. It is just a little known fact that Daddy R. E. told me about that was passe' before I was born and that I had never considered.

"A farmer works from sun to sun." So the little rhyme starts out. That's the way it used to be. Today with the advent of mechanized agriculture and improved lighting, it is nothing to spend 12 to 14 hours or more in the seat of a tractor. The tractor doesn't mind; it is just an unfeeling piece of iron powered by diesel fuel. But what about the days before the wide-spread use of mechanization? In those days we were dependent on animals for power, usually mules.

There are people today that considered the use of draught animals inhuman with a high potential for the abuse of the animals. They generally don't consider that the farmer's livelihood depended on those mules. It was not in the farmer's best interest to mistreat his animals. On our farm just before mechanization, each worker had two teams of mules. They would work one pair in the morning and then switch to a second pair for the afternoon in order to rest the first pair. The farmer might have worked from sun to sun, but the mules only worked part-time.

A MULE TALE, NOT TAIL

This one has nothing to do with family, but this author doubts you ever heard a tale like it.

We have all seen dogs riding in cars, heads hug out the window, mouth open, tongue dangling, wind rushing through their fir, and they just loved the ride. They were the same way when they rode in the back of pickup trucks. But if you happened to be standing in the yard of Newsoms Elementary School in the 1960s, every once and a while an old pickup would go by with an equally old mule standing in the truck bed, head out over the top of the cab looking proudly from side to side at the world that she was sure she owned.

This was Mr. Little and his mule. The first names of both Mr. Little and mule have now escaped me – one of those senior moments. Mr. Little made a living by working or tending gardens for people using his mule. The mule would pull a plow or a drag harrow or a weeding cultivator. Mr. Little and his partner would arrive at a garden site. He would open the tail gate. The mule would descend from the vehicle, get hitched to the implement of the day, work the garden, and get unhitched. With a tap on the tailgate of the pickup and the mule would step into the truck eagerly awaiting her next ride.

So when you think you have seen it all – you ain't.

THE GREAT WAR

I find I am conflicted. I find myself thankful for World War I although millions of people perished in the war. My father, my brothers and sister, my son, my grandson and I are only here because of that war.

Grandmama Edna (Edna Dorothy Hartman) was born in Rockingham County, Virginia, in 1889. Rockingham is in the extreme northwest of the Commonwealth of Virginia. In fact Grandmama Edna's homeplace was at the foot of the Little North Mountain. Go out the back door of the house, climb the mountain for a mile and when you reached the crest of the mountain, you were in West Virginia.

Grandmama was in the first class to graduate from what today is known as James Madison University two years after that institution opened in Harrisonburg. All in that first class graduated with a two year teacher certificate, which at that time was all the Commonwealth of Virginia required to teach grade school.

Somewhere along the way Grandmama fell in love and was to be married to a young man from within the county. Then came World War I and Grandmama's young beau was off to fight with the Army in the Great War. The date is unknown but, at some point during 1918, the young man was killed in the Argonne Forest.

Grandmama Edna was devastated as one might well imagine. She had to get away. Rockingham County held too many reminders of what she had lost. She needed a fresh start. So she picked a place as far away from her home as she could get and still be in Virginia where her teaching certificate was valid. From her childhood home in the far northwest county of Rockingham one mile from the West Virginia state line, she relocated across the state to the far southeastern county of Southampton, taking a room with a family at Sands in a house a scant two miles from the Virginia/North Carolina state line. Grandmama Edna took a position as a teacher at the little two room school there at Sands. The school was located just across the road from Barnes Methodist Church and was within walking distance from the home in which she roomed. I grew up with an entire generation of the older locals calling my grandmother "Miss Hartman."

Grandmama attended services at Barnes and that is where she met Rufus Edwards Drake –Granddaddy Rufus. (Although she attended Barnes Methodist Church for 55 years, and taught Sunday school for years, she continued her membership with Singer's Glenn Baptist Church in Rockingham, leaving them money to purchase hymnals in her will.) Edna and Rufus were married in 1922 and remained so until her death 53 years later. Daddy R. E. was their only child, being born in 1924.

Had her young man from Rockingham not been killed in WWI, Grandmama would have probably lived her whole life in Rockingham. She would not have moved to Southampton County, or met and married granddaddy – no son and no grandchildren here. We owe a lot to the Great War. Fate is fickle, and each and every one of us is a result of a series of countless random events.

SISSY

Grandmama Edna grew up in a family in which 9 children survived to maturity - 8 girls and a lone son. It could be that all of the girls had hearing impediments, but only when they were around each other. Whenever any two or more of them got together, the conversations got very loud and very fast. Excitable might be a better word. But the really odd thing was they all addressed each other as Sissy and all of them talked at the same time. It was possible to have four or five Sissies in the room at the same time having four or five different conversations.

Granddaddy Rufus's house was located on a low hill some hundred and fifty yards from the state maintained road. Once when her sister Emma came to visit, Grandmama called for us boys to come up and spend some time with our grand-aunt. My brothers and I walked the short distance from our driveway down the road to the long lane leading to the house. As we turned into the lane we could hear the old ladies cackling "Lawdy Sissy this and Lawdy Sissy that" and it only got louder as we got closer.

Every summer Grandmama would return to Rockingham County to spend some time with her sisters. Sometimes she stayed with Aunt Emma at Singer's Glen, sometimes with Aunt Minnie in Harrisonburg, or she might be in the home of Aunt Annie in Broadway. She usually rode a bus from Franklin to Harrisonburg, and some of us would make the long drive (four hours) to bring her back home. One time it fell to my Daddy R. E. to go retrieve Grandmama Edna and he took his family along. This particular time she was staying with Aunt Annie. After we got into the town of Broadway, Daddy was not sure exactly to which house we needed to go. We were getting late for our supper with Grandmama Edna and our aunts Annie, Minnie, and Emma and Daddy was not sure where he needed to be. Then he had an idea. He stopped the car, shut off the engine, and had us roll down the windows. Sure enough, six houses down on the left, we could hear the jovial voices "Lawdy Sissy this, and Lawdy Sissy that, and Sissy, Sissy no, and Sissy, Sissy oh yes." We had found where we needed to be.

GRANDMAMA EDNA TO THE RESCUE

It was bad. It was really bad. It wasn't grand theft or murder, but it was bad. It was really, really bad – the kind of bad that gets you a big whipping and I was scared. I don't even remember what my transgression was but it was big whipping bad. If we were Catholic, I could have gone to our parish priest and gotten absolution. But we were a Methodist family full of Baptist females. We had something better than a priest – we had Grandmama Edna.

I was scared to go home and receive my inevitable whipping so I went to my place of refuge. I went to Grandmama Edna's house. There the eight year old told his grandmother of his great sin and his fear of parental retribution. Grandmama asked if I knew what I had done wrong and if I was sorry. Of course I was – now that I faced the big whipping. Grandmama told me not to worry, everything would be alright. After all grandchildren can do no wrong. (Now that I am a grandfather, I know that my grandson may not always be right, but he can never do anything wrong.)

Daddy R. E. came to get me and he was mad. I could see my worst fears were to come true. The Big Whipping. And then the voice of salvation.

Grandmama Edna spoke to her 30 something year old son: R. E. don't you spank that boy when you get home. He knows he did wrong, and he is sorry. Now I am your mama and if you spank that boy I am going to spank you.

Now Daddy was really mad but not at me as much as at Grandmama Edna for reminding him grandparent prerogatives supersede parental. I did not get the whipping.

A SAILOR'S TALE

Daddy R. E. spent 1944 and 1945 floating around the Pacific Ocean on a large T2 oil tanker ship. After completing training as a Merchant Marine engine room engineer at Sheepshead Bay, New York, he was put on a troop train for a five day trip from New York to San Francisco. It was there he boarded a new large T2 oil tanker as an oiler in the engine room. The propulsion system of the ship was a modern day marvel for its time. Boilers burned bunker oil to create steam. The steam then drove a turbine which drove a giant generator which in turn powered an equally giant electric motor connected to the propeller drive shaft.

Daddy R. E. would spend the next six months at sea before he set foot again on dry land. His days were an endless cycle of the 12 to 4 watch – 4 hours on watch, 8 hours off-duty over and over again while at sea. When in port or refueling ships at sea, the engine room crew supplied steam to run the oil pumps and to heat the thick bunker oil to make it easier to pump.

The war only touched Daddy three times during the two years he was at sea. Once they spotted a drifting floating mine and were able to avoid it. The Navy armed guard aboard the ship to man the two cannons on the ship (one on the bow and one on the fantail) as well as the anti-aircraft guns took advantage of the opportunity to use the mine for target practice – they missed. While at the anchorage at Ulithi Atoll, Daddy's ship was toward the back of the long line ships comprising the US 5th Fleet. They were anchored between two smaller Navy tankers and were pumping bunker oil into each when general quarters sounded on the Navy ships and the load speaker announced inbound kamikazes. Being off duty for once, he grabbed a life vest and went to fantail to watch the action, thinking he needed to be ready in case some Japanese pilot decided he wanted to see what 3 ½ million gallons of burning bunker oil looked like. He could see the planes in the distance but none ever got close to the tankers.

At some point during the war, the tankers sailed as a staggered group of three. The tankers would fill at the ports, then leave by the same route twelve hours apart. The first ship left Bushehr, Iran, bound for Ulithi Atoll. Twelve hours later Daddy R. E.'s ship sailed. The last ship sailed twelve hours later. The first two ships arrived at the atoll. The third did not. Daddy never could quite understand why that ship did not make it when the others did: a mild form of survivor's guilt.

Fate is fickle.

Note: In 1977 those who served in the Merchant Marine during World War II were given veteran status by an act of Congress. Of the five veteran groups (Army, Navy, Marine Corp, Coast Guard, and Merchant Marine), as a percentage of its members, the Merchant Marine had the highest number of killed in action.

DEFERRED PAYMENT

I started my working career as a service manager in a large (for Virginia) John Deere dealership in the mid-1970s. After a couple of years, I had the additional title of parts manager thrust upon me. It seemed we were on the verge of converting our inventory control system from manual to computer. I was the only one in the organization with any computer experience – and that was very little. As part of my new role, I sometimes worked the parts counter in customer service.

One day I was on the counter when a customer came in. Looks can be deceiving; this fellow had all the markings of a hobo, or homeless person. I knew he was not because, a year of so earlier, I had witnessed him bargain for a mid-size tractor. When the negotiations were complete, I saw him reach into the top pocket of his worn, torn bib overalls and pull out a roll of cash big enough to choke a mule and pay cash for the purchase of the multi-thousand dollar machine. Mid-size John Deere tractors weren't cheap even in the 1970s. I had completed a rather large sale to this man of plow points, disk harrow blades, and other assorted wear type items when the customer says "Can I pay for this after I sell my pigs?" I could see out of the corner of my eye my boss, the dealership owner. with this sly little smile on his face. I knew the ragged hobo had stellar credit with company. So I said "Sure that will be fine" and then as an afterthought I asked "When do you expect to sell them?"

"Ah, hell, I don't know. Ain't bred the sow yet."

COUNTRY EDUCATION TIME AGAIN

Ok, city folks and young'uns, it's country education time again. After this author wrote the above, it occurred to him there were probably some, if not all, who did not get the joke that was played on me. The gestation period for a hog sow is a bit less than four months. From the time a pig is born until it is sold as a feeder pig is two to three months. If selling the pigs as market hogs, six months. What the customer was saying was that it was going to be six months to ten months before we got paid after the sow was impregnated and he offered no time frame for that event to occur. But fear not, the next week a check arrived for the full amount as my boss knew it would.

FRONT OF THE CHURCH, BACK OF THE CHURCH

Country churches can be really confusing: it is the only place I know that when you go through the front door you are at the back of the church. Occasionally it can lead to some Abbot and Costello "Who's on First" situations as witnessed by this author (embellished quite a bit). A member of the church came through the front door and took a seat at the first pew he encountered. It was a sparse crowd for that service and the pastor did not really feel like shouting to make himself heard to a spread out small crowd. So the pastor said to the way-back member.

"Brother so and so, wouldn't you like to come to the front of the church where you can hear better?"

"I am at the front of the church."

"No you are at the back of church."

"How do you figure this is the back of the church?"

"Because the front of the church is where the altar and pulpit are."

"Then where is the front door?"

"Right there behind you."

(pause)

"I have to go relieve myself, where is your in-house?"

By Joe H. Drake

Respectful Disagreement

Any work of a genealogical nature is much like a photograph in that it is a moment frozen in time. The work represents the findings and conclusions of the author based on research that he had available at the time of the writing. The challenge to the author is when to end his research and begin his writing. Consequently, all works of genealogy are subject to revision and alteration if records are uncovered in the future not available previously.

When records are uncovered that prove a previous work may not be as accurate as the author had thought, this should not be thought of as a repudiation of the author's work, but rather a continuation of the author's work. The perfectly accurate work of genealogy of any size has yet to be written. Indeed, such a work may be impossible to write.

Now in Our Fourth Century: Some American Families, by Paul Drake, Heritage Books, copyright 1994, is a remarkable social history of the lives of everyday people in 17th and 18th century America as seen through the lives and genealogy of the ancestors of Paul Drake. Paul's book brings history to the level of the common person in a view seldom seen in ordinary history books: indeed the book is an *extraordinary* work.

On page 158 of his book, Paul states: "The next chapter of this work is missing. It should be entitled 'Drury and Sarah (Sary) Kitchen Drake.' However, and again despite our best efforts, we know little of those ancestors." Without a doubt, to say information on Drury (spelled Drewry in those times) is scarce is unquestionably true.

During the period 1790 – 1830, there appeared two households with Drewrys as the head. One was in Edgecombe County, NC; the other in Southampton County, VA. In both households there appeared a son named Drewry (or Drury). The family of Drewry of Edgecombe has family ties to the Drakes of Southampton in that Drewry of Edgecombe had three uncles who lived there, brothers of his father Lazarus.

Given the duplication of the name of the head of household, the duplication of the name of a son, and the fact that Drewry of Edgecombe had such close ties to the Drake family of Southampton, it is reasonable to assume the families are one and the same. As Paul wrote in his book: "The answer seems to be that Drue maintained two households, one in Southampton, in which his children and an elder member of the family resided, and a second in Edgecombe, in which he and Sarah lived, and from which he earned his livelihood."

If one were to set out with the sole goal of trying to disprove the one Drewry, two household theory, he would probably fail. Nevertheless, it is now believed the theory has fatal flaws – discovered by chance.

While abstracting deeds in the Southampton County Courthouse of which his 4x great-grandfather, Thomas Barnes, was a party, the writer of this thesis came upon the following deed.

Southampton County Deed Book 21, Page 369
George Artis, free Negro
To
Thomas Barnes
Drewry Drake, trustee
Deed made August 11, 1830, recorded August 11, 1830

Deed of Trust: Debt to Thomas Barnes, $7.00. Lien on all furniture in house, crop lien on corn and cotton crop, 8 hogs, 1 plough, 2 plough hoes, 2 coulters.

Signed:
George (his X mark) Artis
Thomas (his seal) Barnes
Drewry (his X mark) Drake
No witnesses

In his book, Paul states that Drewry was literate and gives two examples. The first, Drewry signs his name as a witness to his brother's will in Edgecombe, NC; the other, Drewry's signature on a deed where he sells his reversionary interest to the farm in Edgecombe left to him by his father upon the death of his mother Sarah Hines. The Drewry in Southampton, as evidenced by this deed, was unable to write his name. This suggests not one Drewry with two households, but rather two Dreweys: one in Edgecombe County, North Carolina, and the other in Southampton County, Virginia.

But one x on a deed does not necessarily constitute proof. Other examples followed while researching collateral lines.

Southampton County Deed Book 13, Page 291
Rueben Whitfield and Phele, his wife
To
Stephen Barnes
Deed made June 24, 1813, recorded June 24, 1813

Deed of Trust to cover debt of $395. Lien on specified lands. Jacob Barnes, trustee.
Signed:
Rueben (his seal) Whitfield
Phele (her seal) Whitfield
Stephen (his X mark) Barnes
Witness: James (his seal) Jones, William (his X mark) Newsom,
Drewry (his X mark) Drake

While researching the neighbors of Jesse Drake, this writer's 5x great-grandfather, the will of one John Jackson was encountered in Southampton County Will Book 5, Page 376, recorded January 7, 1803. Again, Drewry was a witness, as well as Sally Drake, probably Sarah Kitchen, Drewry's wife. While deeds are presented, copied, and returned to the owner, wills are permanently filed in the clerk's office. After much explaining to the clerk and two hours of searching, the fragile 201-year-old document was located and carefully unfolded enough to copy the page of witnesses. It clearly shows the marks of both Drewry (X) and Sally (S) (Sarah) Drake. Note: When this will is viewed in Will Book 5, the name Drewry Beal is shown as a witness. Drewry Beal is also named the executor of the estate of John Jackson. Below the hand-written copy of the will is the certification of the court. This certification states the will was approved by the court upon the oath of Drewry Drake, witness. Had it not been for this inconsistency, the clerk of the court probably would never have agreed to allow the search of the fragile wills themselves, which proved a two-century-old transcription error in the recordation of the witness.

If one were to read the transcription of the 1790 census for Edgecombe County, NC, he would find a listing for a Henry Drake household having one male over 16 years of age, two males less than 16 years of age, and a female. This Henry never existed. A check of the images of this census reveals that he who was transcribed as Henry is actually Drewry. This is two years before the Drewry in Southampton married Sarah Kitchen.

In his book, Paul states that in 1836 Drury, Jr., the son of Drury of Southampton and Drury, Jr.'s brother, William Kitchen Drake (the ancestor of Paul) left Southampton to go west. William settled in Ohio. Drury, Jr. went on to eventually settle in Illinois.

In the 1860 census, Drury, Jr. can be found as a 47-year-old white male, born in Virginia and living in Senachwine Township, Putnam County, Illinois. This indicates a birth year for Drury, Jr., son of Drewry of Southampton, of about 1812 – 1813.

Paul states in his book that Sarah Hines Drake, mother of Drewry of Edgecomb made her nuncupative will in March of 1804. The will was recorded on March 19, 1804, indicating the death of Sarah sometime before that date. In her will she directs that her clothes, or as many that could be cut to fit, be left to Drury, Jr., son of Drewry of Edgecomb (see *Now In Our Fourth Century: Some American Families* by Paul Drake, page 158).

Obviously, Sarah Hines Drake would not make a legacy to a grandson who was not to be born until nine years later. This is a very good indication, but probably absolute proof, that there were two Drury, Jr.s. and, therefore, two older Drewrys: one in Southampton and one in Edgecombe.

Oddly, this 1860 census record was sent to this writer by Paul Drake, who probably failed to recognize its significance.

In his will Lazarus Drake, the father of Drewry of Edgecomb and husband of Sarah Hines Drake, left his Edgecombe plantation to Sarah as a life estate with a reversionary interest to Drewry. Sarah sold her life estate and Drewry sold his reversionary interest to this plantation in by a deed dated July 9, 1799. This deed exhibits no provisions for the dower interests of the wife of Drewry. This strongly suggests that Drewry of Edgecombe was either unmarried or a widower at the time. Drewry of Southampton had been married to Sarah Kitchen seven years at this time and would continue to be married to her for another 16 to 25 years.

Conclusion: With all due respect to Paul Drake, superb genealogist, accomplished author, distant cousin, and dear friend, there were two Drewry Drakes. One the son of Lazarus Drake living in Edgecombe County, North Carolina; the other living in Southampton County, Virginia. The information given in Paul's book is a combination of the two.

The information that follows is the product of this writer and Dr. Charles E. Drake of Savannah, GA., a friend, cousin, and research collaborator.

Who were the parents of Drewry of Southampton? At this time, this cannot be answered conclusively, but there is some evidence that gives us indications. Based on this evidence, it is felt that Jesse Drake and his wife, Ann, are the probable parents of Drewry of Southampton. The parents of Ann, wife of Jesse, have yet to be absolutely identified, but the evidence suggests her father was Jeremiah Ellis.

The parents of Jesse Drake are John Drake and his first wife, Mary Browne, daughter of Dr. Samuel Browne (see note 1). In his will Dr. Browne names Mary as his daughter and the wife of John Drake. He wills her a 500-acre plantation during her life with a reversionary interest to her oldest son Jesse. In addition, Jesse is also left a 300-acre tract. John Drake (2) is the oldest brother of Lazarus Drake, thus one of the three uncles of Drewry of Edgecombe living in Southampton.

Jesse Drake was born about 1723 (3) and died testate in 1773. In his will (Southampton County Will Book 3, Page 51) Jesse leaves his movables to his wife, Ann, during her life or widowhood. Then they are to be divided amongst "all my children". Those children are believed to be: Jeremiah born about 1760, Drewry born about 1765, Elizabeth born about 1768, Dorothy born about 1770, and Polly born about 1771.

No record has been found to date that names the children of Jesse and Ann Drake. Identification was made by analyzing what records there were available and, while these placements are not proven, they are highly probable. We are greatly aided in these placements by the fact that the family of John and Mary Browne Drake were the only family of Drakes on the St. Luke's Parish side of the Nottoway River for nearly a century. The lower Nottoway River in Southampton County, Virginia, is wide – 200 to 300 yards. The Drake lands were on the lower Nottoway. The nearest bridge across the river at that time would have been Cypress Bridge about 12 miles up river. For young people of courting age, the lower Nottoway proved to be a formidable obstacle. Thus the vast majority St. Luke's younger generations in the 1700's married other young people of St. Luke's Parish.

John Drake had a total of eight sons (4), by two wives, six of whom survived to maturity. Of these six sons, all had moved away except Jesse by the time the children of Jesse were of age to marry.

Of the five proposed children of Jesse and Ann, Jeremiah is the most definite child for, under the primogenitor laws in effect at the time, he inherited the land (5).

On February 2, 1790, Elizabeth Drake wed William Bradley. Surety was provided by Jeremiah (6). The Personal Property Tax Lists show William Bradley as a tithable in the household of Ann Drake. From this it can safely be assumed that Elizabeth is a child of Jesse and Ann Drake.

From combining the age data from the 1810, 1820, and 1830 censuses for Southampton County, it can be determined that Dorothy was born about 1770. She evidently lived her entire life in the area close to the Drake lands in St. Luke's Parish, for in 1796, she was a witness to the nuncupative will of one Henry Ellis who died in the home of Jacob Vick, a neighbor of Jesse and Ann. Dorothy married Thomas Barnes who through the years had numerous dealings with Jeremiah and Drewry Drake after his marriage to Dorothy. From this, and the fact that there was no other Drake in the area who could have been her father, it is felt that Dorothy is a child of Jesse and Ann Drake.

Polly Drake married Newit Edwards on or about October 20, 1800. Providing surety for the marriage was either Jeremiah's brother-in-law or father-in-law, George Gurley (the record does not state if this was George Gurley, Sr. or Jr.) (7). This placement is a bit less sure than the others. The lands of Newit Edwards were approximately 1 to 2 miles west of the Nottoway River and the lands of the Drakes. As Jesse Drake's clan was the only Drakes anywhere near, it is probable that he is the father of Polly.

Drewry first appears in the records of Southampton in the tax list of 1791, oddly enough in Nottoway Parish. It is not known why he should be in Nottoway Parish when his father and grandfather lived in St. Luke's Parish on an 800-acre plantation given by the will of Samuel Browne to his daughter, Mary Browne Drake, and grandson Jesse. Perhaps, as he was young when his father died, Drewry went to live and help one or both of the younger brothers of his grandfather John. Thomas and William both lived in Nottoway Parish, neither had any known male heirs, and both lived well into their eighties. Perhaps he was living with kin of his mother Ann. Whatever the reason, Drewry was listed in the tax lists for Nottoway Parish for the years 1791, 1792, and 1793. (8)

In 1794 Ann, widow of Jesse, disappears from the tax list. The implications are she died in late 1793 or early 1794. In 1794 Drewry also disappears from the tax list of Nottoway Parish. In 1794 Jeremiah, oldest son of Jesse and Ann, gains a tithable although his oldest son is less than 15 years old. It is quite possible that upon the death of Ann, Drewry moved back across the Nottoway River to the place of his birth to farm what had been the dower lands of Ann and was taxed as part of brother Jeremiah's household.

The tax list parallels continue:

In 1798, Drewry gains a slave on the tax list.
In 1798, Jeremiah loses a slave on the tax list.

In 1799, Drewry loses a slave on the tax list.
In 1799, Jeremiah gains a slave on the tax list.

In 1800, Drewry gains a slave on the tax list.
In 1800, Jeremiah loses a slave on the tax list.

In 1805, Drewry gains 3 horses on the tax lists.
In 1805, Jeremiah loses 5 horses on the tax lists.

In 1806, Drewry loses 3 horses on the tax lists.
In 1806, Jeremiah gains 5 horses on the tax lists. (9)

These are indications that Drewry and Jeremiah had a very close relationship. It should be noted that under the laws of primogenitor in effect at the time, the oldest son Jeremiah inherited all the lands of his father Jesse.

Considering naming patterns as an indication, Drewry named a son Jeremiah. He also named a daughter Nancy, often a nickname for Ann (his mother).

Drewry's proposed sister, Dorothy, married Thomas Barnes, he of the deed of trust mentioned earlier. Drewry seems to have had several business dealings with either Thomas or his younger brother Jacob. During the period of 1794 to 1830 and beyond, Drewry and most of his offspring were living on the lands of Jeremiah or (after the death of Jeremiah in 1811) the lands of Thomas Barnes and/or his brother Jacob (or in some cases one of their Barnes or Pope nephews of whom Dorothy would have been their aunt by marriage).

And finally, it should be noted again that the family of John and Mary Browne Drake for 100 years were the only Drakes on the St. Luke's side of the Nottoway River in Southampton County. This severely limits the number of other possibilities.

Taken as a whole, these indications make a body of evidence that, while not definite, is fairly clear and convincing that Drewry of Southampton is a son of Jesse and Ann Drake.

NOTES

1. Isle of Wight County, Virginia. Will Book 4, Page 274 dated October 17, 1739, recorded June 23, 1740
2. John is assumed to be the oldest as he was the first to be mentioned in the will of his father Thomas (TD) Drake, and as he is the first to be mentioned in any record regarding him or his brothers, and is a signer of the "petition of 1722" which indicates he was of age i.e. born before 1701. His brothers are Thomas, William and Lazarus.
3. Dr. Browne's will of 1739 seems to indicate that Jesse was of age, or very close to being 21 at that time. Of the grandchildren mentioned by Dr. Browne, Jesse was the only one whose legacy was not limited by the term "when of age". (From the notes of Dr. Charles E. Drake, here after CED)
4. Will of John Drake, Southampton Will Book 2, Page 361, recorded December 13, 1770.
5. Southampton County Land Books, 1782 – 1850.
6. Southampton County Marriage Register, page 64.
7. Southampton County Marriage Register, page 138.
8. Personal property tax list for Southampton County 1782 – 1850. (CED)
9. Excerpted from the tax lists by Joe H. Drake

Finding the Parents of

Susan Edwards

Building the Case for Clear and Convincing

There is no single record or records that definitively state the names of the parents of Susan Edwards. This essay will detail the process by which her parents were determined. The process starts by inventorying what is known by the records available. According to the marriage bond for Susan and James E. Drake (Southampton County, Virginia, marriage bond register, page 513), Susan's age on 21 December 1841, was 21 so she was born in 1820. However, in the census of 1850 onward, the age she gives would mean she was born in 1821. In all the censuses, she always stated she was born in Virginia.

The world of 1840 was one which basically traveled at a rate of three miles per hour. This brings about the question of how long and how far would James E. Drake go to court Susan. A reasonable estimate would be about five miles – nearly two hours. Certainly it would be doubtful he traveled more than ten miles or about three hours. So we can safely surmise that Susan would have lived in St. Luke's parish, which is on the southwest side of the Nottoway River.

Examining all the Edwards households in Southampton (both St. Luke's and Nottaway parishes) for the census years of 1830 and 1840 shows only two which have females in the same age range as Susan, both of which are in St. Luke's parish. The two households are those of Peter Edwards who resided in the area between present day Boykins and Capron (about 8-9 miles from James's home at Piney Woods, today known as Sands) and Peterson Edwards who was in the Sunbeam-Mt. Horeb area (about 4-5 miles). Peterson Edwards died intestate. Peter Edwards left a will and named a daughter not named Susan. In fact, in checking all the Edwards wills in Southampton County who could have been of age to be the parent of Susan, none listed a daughter by the name of Susan.

> Note that in the census of 1830 and 1840 only the head of household is listed by name. All others in the home are denoted by only their sex and age range i.e.: 0-5, 6-10, and so on.

The minister who married Susan Edwards and James E. Drake was Robert S. Barnes. Robert was an associate minister of Barnes Methodist Church and a founder and first trustee of Mt. Horeb Methodist Church, which may be an indication that Susan's home was relatively near James's. Robert S. Barnes and James's mother Dorothy Barnes Drake would have been first cousins.

The first born child of James and Susan was Thomas Harrison Drake who was born in November of 1842. Thomas named his first child by his second wife, Caroline Burgess, Peter. At least we know he was called Peter. His name might have well been Peterson. Either way, Peter or Peterson, it is a good indication that his grandfather was Peterson Edwards. Up until this time, there had never been a Drake in Southampton with the name Peter. Nor has any Burgess, up to that time, been found with the name Peter. (The author is fairly confident he has found all the Drakes in the county up to that time and a bit beyond – the Burgesses not so much so.)

Peterson Edwards married Polly Browne on the first day of December, 1813. The minister who married them was Benjamin Barnes. Benjamin Barnes was an ordained minister and elder of the Methodist Church. He was also the father of Robert S. Barnes and grand-uncle of James E. Drake – a brother to James's grandfather Thomas Barnes. Benjamin lived on his farm which was adjacent to the farm inherited by James and his brother William Drake from their grandfather Thomas. This illustrates that the families of James E. Drake and those of Susan Edwards lived in the same area for at least two generations and were familiar with each other.

In summary, the families of Peterson Edwards and the families of James E. Drake were in relatively close proximity to each other. The families were familiar with each other. In the census of 1830 and 1840, Peterson Edwards is the only Edwards family in Southampton County with a daughter the age of Susan. Thomas Harrison Drake, the son of James E. and Susan, named a son Peter most likely after Thomas Harrison's grandfather. (Thomas Harrison Drake would have been in his early teens when Peterson Edwards passed away so he would have been quite familiar with him.) Given the above and the fact no other Edwards families have been found, it becomes obvious, clear, and convincing that Peterson Edwards and Polly Browne are the parents of Susan Edwards.

The Sermon

If you read the first paragraph of the first chapter, you know I promised not to preach at you. I lied, but only by a small amount, and this could be important. I'll keep it short.

The vast majority of the stories and tales relayed in this narrative are from about the Civil War period and forward in time. That is because they were oral history relayed to the author by older generations who had either first or second hand knowledge of what they were speaking. As far as I know, none of it was ever written down until now. That is all well and good for the now, but what about all those who came before? Where are their stories and antidotes to reveal the character of our ancestors? Those tales died with the people who knew them. They did not record them yesterday so that we might have them today.

It saddens me to know that we will never know what made our "however many greats" before the word grandparents laugh or cry. Or what they loved and disliked. How they felt about what was happening in the world around them. Why they might have done this or not have done that. How they survived in this world. What moral lessons did they want to pass on to the next generations? Many could not read or write so they have to be forgiven. I wish the others would have left a note or two.

A large part of what we as genealogists and family historians do is document archeology. The problem with documents is that, in time, the few non-government types that might have told us something of the character of our ancestors slowly erode away, leaving only the cold government records of taxes, census, marriage bonds, deeds and wills. Occasionally one might glean a bit of personality from a will but the information is usually very scant. It is hard to imagine an ancestor's smile from a number on a census page.

Paul Drake, if I have figured correctly, is a third cousin once removed - kin, but only barely. Paul wrote a book entitled "*You Ought to Write That Down*". It goes into great detail about recording family history, not just genealogy. The difference? Family history has personality in it rather than just the cold hard facts of genealogy. Personality is just that – personal. It separates us from one another; it makes us unique individuals. Family history is largely about personality and is far more interesting than plain genealogy: it allows us to use mental imagery.

The point? All us have information that our children and grandchildren will want to pass on to their children and grandchildren. Certainly, you do not owe them the story of their heritage, but it would surely make them a wonderful gift. Find a way to pass on your history. I tried to.

Rendezvous with History

(Or where micro-history collides with macro-history)

This is not the way this section should begin, with a historical/genealogical mystery rather than with known and proven facts. But, chronologically, this is the earliest item on the list so this is where we start.

On May 13, 1607, three ships arrived at a peninsula on the north shore of the James River. The 104 men and boys who came ashore founded the first permanent English colony in North America. They called their settlement "Jamestowne". One of those earliest colonists was a young carpenter named John Laydon. In 1608, more settlers arrived from England. Among these was Ann Burras, the maidservant of the wife of Thomas Forrest. Some accounts state that Ann was about 17 at the time, some say as young as 14. The first marriage between English settlers in North America occurred when John Laydon and Ann Burras were wed. We can only imagine the trials and tribulations the young couple must have endured. They survived the Starving Time of 1609 when only 60 people of about 490 survived[1]. They survived the 1622 Good Friday massacre, when at least 357 people - one third of the colonists - were killed by Indians. The Laydons can be found in the 1624 muster, living along Warwick Creek in what today would be Newport News with their four daughters, the youngest of whom was named Alice. Note: of the 104 men and boys who first established Jamestown in 1607, only two were listed in the Muster of 1624.

Supposedly, Alice Laydon married Thomas Willoughby, also listed on the Muster of 1624, and the couple moved to his land holdings across the James River in what today would be Norfolk. The Willoughbys seem to have been prosperous and influential up until the time of the Revolution. The Revolution threatened the social and financial order of the colony - a social and financial order by which the Willoughbys had been successful. The family remained loyal to the crown and would come to be known as Tories. As the Revolution wore on, the Willoughbys became less and less welcome around the Norfolk area and they found it advisable to relocate to the interior of North Carolina.

About this time, 1776 – 1780, the first known references to the name Willoughby can be found in Hertford County, North Carolina. These Willoughbys were located in the southeast section of the county near present day Ahoskie and the Bertie County line. The Questions: Are the Willoughbys of Hertford County, North Carolina, the same family as the relocated Willoughbys of Norfolk, Virginia (a distance between the two locals of 50 – 60 miles)? Can the line of Willoughbys be established from the Revolution back to Thomas Willoughby, he of the Muster of 1624? And can it be established that Thomas Willoughby did indeed marry Alice Laydon? If these questions can be answered in the affirmative, then a considerable number of people will be able to trace their heritage back to the very first settlers of our nation.

The 357 people - men, women, and children - killed and the 20 women taken captive by Indians in the Good Friday Massacre of 1622 were more than King James I could tolerate. He revoked the charter of the Virginia Company and Virginia became a royal colony as the company was practically insolvent as it was. The Virginia Company had been a private stock company formed to explore and exploit England's claims in North America. It is not known if any of the investors ever recovered any part of their investment. Now that King James had a colony, he had to discover what it was he had. To that end he ordered an inventory of the firearms, swords, other weapons, tools

---

[1] The Starving Time was in large part due to the Jamestown fort being under siege by the Powhatan Indians. No person could leave the confines of the fort to hunt or fish without being killed. What is little known is that there were one or two small pockets or outposts of settlers at other places and these were ignored by the Indians. One of these was at Old Point Comfort where the James River meets the Chesapeake Bay. These settlers were free to hunt and fish and were largely unaware of the plight of the fort. It is probable that John and Ann Burras Laydon were among the few settlers at Old Point Comfort.

and livestock and he had all the people listed along with where they were located. This became known as the Muster of 1624. Of the 1,033 persons enumerated, one, John Upton, is known to be listed in this work. Edward Barnes, another listed in the Muster is also believed to probably be the same person by that name listed within this work. In addition, there is a John Burrow listed in the Muster who might be the John Barrow born circa 1609 who is part of this research guide.

Of the three known or thought to be in the muster, the most is known about John Upton. According to a blog found in the Jamestown Settlement website, Upton came to Virginia as an indentured servant in 1620. He purchased the remaining time on his indenture contract in 1622 and became a free man. After the Muster of 1624 he moved across the James River into Isle of Wight where he, over the years, became a captain of the militia and accumulated a large land holding, some of which was gained by manipulation of the headright system. See the narrative "*Random Thoughts and Observations*" for a closer look at the headright system in general and John Upton's use of it in particular.

About 1620, an orphan boy by the name Edward Barnes was ordered transported to Virginia by the court in London. A short time later, Edward Barnes shows up in the records as an indentured servant. This all fits in nicely with what is known of Edward Barnes of early Isle of Wight County. That, coupled with the fact that no other records of any other Edward Barnes found to date, leads us to believe that Edward Barnes of Isle of Wight, and Edward Barnes the indentured servant of the Muster of 1624, and Edward Barnes the boy ordered to be transported by the court in London are all the same person.

There is a John Barrow listed in this research guide. There is a John Burrow listed in the Muster of 1624. It is not known when John Barrow came to Virginia, nor is it known under what circumstances he came to Virginia. It is only known that Barrow died in Surry County about 1680, leaving a will naming his wife and two sons. Of the John Burrow listed in the Muster of 1624, nothing is known other than he was in Virginia in 1624. The two Johns would have been of similar age. The difference in the spelling of the last name means very little as at that time few people could read and write and those that could generally spelled names phonetically. See the "*Introduction*" for an explanation on the spellings of names. John Barrow and John Burrow could be the same person.

Nathaniel Bacon was the spark needed to ignite a rebellion in 1676. It has been said that Bacon was a hundred years ahead of his time. Young, impulsive, bold and charismatic, Bacon was just the sort who could rally the discontent of the poorer people into action. The causes of the discontent among the growing class of former indentured servants are many. The Navigation Acts passed by the English Parliament dictated that all export items from the colonies had to be transported by English ship to England, and exports from the colonies were to be taxed. All the items imported into the colonies were also to be by English ships bound from England. England created a monopoly by which the colonies were plundered. With no competition from the Dutch or French traders, the price for tobacco and other Virginia-produced products plummeted. The cost of goods needed from abroad soared. The small farmers/former indentured servants were affected the most from this as they could least afford the charges.

Although the former indentured servants were entitled to small plots of land, where they could find such land was limited. King Charles II had given all of the Carolinas and the Northern Neck of Virginia to his friends. William Penn gained all of Pennsylvania as payment of a debt owed to his father by the English Crown. Much of the lands were off-limits in order not to further alienate the Indians by whom the elite of the colony were being enriched via the fur trade.

There was no redress of the grievances of the people through the elected Burgesses or the courts. Governor William Berkeley had not allowed free elections of the Burgesses or courts in sixteen years. And over that span of time, all the courts in all the counties had been packed with his appointees and supporters. And finally, all along the frontiers of the colony there were incursions by the Indians, resulting in the loss of life and property of the colonists. In most cases the colonist were not allowed to respond.

Isle of Wight and Surry Counties of 1676 was no different than the other counties of the colony. There were few roads, and those roads that did exist were little more than paths. Most of the commerce and communications was by the waterways to the James River and from there to Jamestown or one of the towns further downriver. The dilemma of the settlers of Isle of Wight and Surry was that eight to ten miles inland from the James River the water courses no longer flow north to the James but south into North Carolina and eventually to the Albemarle Sound, restricting commerce at that time to the eight miles or so inland from the James. From that point to the south, Isle of Wight was the frontier (complete with Native American tribes who also at times were a problem) and so the Government in Jamestown sought to limit growth into that area. But there were former indentured servants and the Quakers who desired to go south deeper into Isle of Wight and they were not happy about the restrictions as the further they could get from the colonial authorities the better.

To make a long story short and encapsulate a whole revolution in one paragraph, after a provocation by Indians in New Kent County, Nathaniel Bacon raised a small force of willing men to chastise the offenders without permission of either the Governor or the House of Burgesses. Governor Berkeley was furious and raised his own band of militia to oppose Bacon. Rather than disband his force, Bacon marched on Jamestown forcing Berkeley to flee to the more hospitable Eastern Shore. Bacon burned Jamestown. By this time many if not most of the indentured servants, both current and former had rallied to the side of Bacon. Most of the rich planters either evacuated the area or tried to remain neutral. The rebellion died when Bacon died of malaria (some sources say dysentery). Berkeley returned with soldiers sent from England. Note that the only recorded deaths (Native Americans excluded) from this uprising occurred when Governor Berkeley hanged twenty-three of the rebels. It has not been found if any of the twenty-three were afforded a trial. King Charles II commented that Berkeley ("that old fool") had hanged more men for this little uprising than he (the King) had hanged for the murder of his father, Charles I. William Berkeley was recalled to England and a new Governor was appointed.

Meanwhile in Isle of Wight, supporters of Bacon had seized the mansion home of Arthur Allen located in Surry very near the boundary with Isle of Wight to hold for the use of Bacon and his men. The home has come down through history to be known as "Bacon's Castle". It is most probable that some, if not all, of these men are the same ones who petitioned the King's Commissioners for a pardon (which was granted) for their part in the rebellion. Among those who signed the petition are John (J.) Drake, Peter Hayes (Haise), Thomas Carter, Carter's father-in-law George Moore, and his brother Thomas Moore. These five are very probably the same as can be found in this research guide. In addition, if the estimated birth years are off by only a few years, George Hill, John Davis, and John Harris found in this work may have also been involved in the rebellion and requested a pardon by the same petition.

Some good did come of the rebellion. William Berkeley, who was proving to be somewhat of a tyrant in his old age, was recalled as Governor. Expeditions were organized against offending Indians (as well as some who had offended no one), regular elections of the House of Burgesses were resumed, all free men were given the right to vote instead of just the land owners, and the number of persons on the local courts were greatly reduced. Those that remained were to be elected by the free men of the counties. New lands were made available for settlement. Note that all of the above mentioned Isle of Wight men would settle in the newly opened area of Isle of Wight from which in 1749 Southampton County would be created.

Colonial Isle of Wight was divided into two parishes, Upper Parish and Lower Parish. With the formation of Southampton County in 1749, two other parishes were created: Nottoway Parish, which consisted of the area between the Blackwater and the Nottoway Rivers, and St. Luke's Parish, which was all the area from the south of the Nottoway to the North Caroline line. The Church of England required that its ministers in the New World be educated and ordained in England or, after 1707, Great Britain. This led to a lack of clergy to service the outlying areas, such as, the Lower Parish of Isle of Wight and all of early Southampton. The Methodist Church was in large part a result of the Great Awakening which reached the southern colonies around 1760. From its inception the Methodist Church was meant to be a part of the established church, that being the Church of England, and also required its ministers to be ordained in England. The American Revolution changed that. The Methodists became a totally separate denomination and the Church of England in the new United States became the Episcopal Church.

Listed below are some, but probably not all, of the early (prior to 1860) ministers who can be found in this research Guide:

Robert Bracewell, born circa (c) 1618 – Little is known of Robert other than his son Richard Braswell lived and died in Isle of Wight. Robert was probably Church of England (aka Anglican or Episcopalian). No record has been found that he ever left England.

Thomas Burgess (Burges), born c1720 – Church of England. He served Southampton for a time until he relocated to Halifax County, North Carolina, in 1759.

George Gurley, born c1725 – Native to Isle of Wight. His father was also George Gurley, born c1698. The younger George went off to England to be educated and ordained as a minister of the Church of England and returned to serve Southampton.

Henry John Burgess, born c1744 – The son of Rev. Thomas Burgess was a minister with the Anglican or Episcopal Church as was his father. Served Southampton for a time, but it is not known for how long or where he was before or after his Southampton time.

Joseph Gurley, born c1746 – The son of Rev. George Gurley (Jr.) replaced his father as rector of St. Luke's Parish and Vick's Old Church located a mile east of Newsoms, Va. To ensure that the reader is sufficiently confused, St. Luke's Church is in Nottoway Parish. It sits on the north bank of the Nottoway River so, from the church's cemetery, one can look across the river from St. Luke's Church to St. Luke's Parish. St. Luke's Church seems to have served both parishes as the author has yet to find any reference to any other Episcopal church in Southampton County.

Exum Everett, born c1753 – An assistant or local minister at Barnes Methodist Church. In the early Methodist Church, ordained ministers had many churches to which they made regular visits but there were far too many churches to minister to every Sunday. These traveling reverends became known as circuit riders. Assistant or local ministers were left to serve the church when the ordained minister or circuit rider was elsewhere. Some of the assistant ministers may have been fully ordained, some were not. It is not known if Exum Everett was ever ordained although he performed many wedding services as evidenced by his minister's returns in the Southampton County marriage register. During the week, he was a farmer like all his neighbors. See the narrative "*The Founding and Founders of Barnes Methodist Church*"

Joel Drake, born c1755 – Supposedly he was a Revolutionary soldier who witnessed the surrender of Lord Cornwallis at Yorktown. He migrated west with his brother Jordan and founded a Methodist Church in Warren County, Ohio.

Richard W. Drake, born c1755, in ether Southampton County, Virginia, or Halifax County, North Carolina - It is not known exactly when his father Tristam Drake relocated. Richard was a Revolutionary veteran and was a Methodist minister in Chatham County, North Carolina.

Benjamin Barnes, born c1763 – A fully ordained minister and elder of the Methodist Church, he rode several circuits until he returned to Southampton, the county of his birth, to help establish Barnes Methodist Church which was located on his father's (Jacob) land. He, along with Exum Everett, were two of the first trustees of Barnes Methodist Church. See the narrative "*The Founding and Founders of Barnes Methodist Church*"

Note: Often when reading about the early churches prior to the Revolution, the term "meeting house" is used to describe the building. This is because at that time there was only one church, that being the Church of England, and to refer to other sects or their church buildings as churches could be considered treason. The habit of calling non Church of England buildings meeting houses continued into the early 1800s.

Newit Vick, born c1765 – A Methodist minister, it is not known if he was fully ordained. He migrated from Southampton to Mississippi where in 1825 he founded the town of Vicksburg, Mississippi.

George Gurley (III), born c1765 – This is another son of the Rev. George Gurley; however, unlike his father and older brother, the younger George served the Methodist Church. He is listed as the main minister at Barnes Methodist Church for 30 years, 1808 to 1838.

Francis Williamson, born c1773 – Very little is known of Rev. Francis Williamson other than he was born in Southampton and died in Murfreesboro, NC. His daughter married into the Bryant family. Francis married Elizabeth Worrell, daughter of Richard Worrell of Southampton County. Two of the known sons of Francis and Elizabeth also became ministers: Rev. Elijah Williamson, born 1804, and Rev. James Williamson, born 1806. It is not now known where these sons preached or which denomination they represented.

Ethelbert Drake, born c1788 – He was a son of Rev. Richard W. Drake. Ethelbert was a minister in Richmond, Virginia, where he founded the *Virginia Advocate* Newspaper which was taken over by the Virginia Methodist Conference when Ethelbert became insolvent. The *Virginia Advocate* became, and is today, the journal of the Virginia Methodist Conference.

Simon Murfree, born 23 June 1788 - Son of Simon Murfree (Sr.), there is not much known of the Rev. Murfree other than references calling him Reverend. In his history of Southampton County, Thomas Parramore states that Rev. Murfree was the minister of South Quay Baptist Church.

Davis Bryant, born c1795 – Methodist Minister of Barnes Methodist Church, he was probably a local minister; however, the Barnes records list him as the main pastor for 1848 and 1849. Bryant had 13 children and, upon his death, he left each of them a farm.

William H. Drake, born 1796. He was another son of Rev .Richard W. Drake and the brother of Ethelbert Drake. One notation has been found stating that William was a Methodist minister but, at this time, it is not known if he was fully ordained or a local minister or where or when he might have preached.

Joshua Leigh, born c1800 – Leigh was a circuit rider as a minister in the Virginia Methodist Conference. He was the minister at Barnes Methodist Church, 1838-1840, with Robert S. Barnes as his assistant minister. He married Charlotte Harris Musgrave, the widow of Dr. Richard Thomas Musgrave who died in 1837. Joshua Leigh left a journal, now in the possession of the Southampton Historical Society, in which he names many members of the various local Methodist Churches.

Robert S. Barnes, born c1804 – A son of the Rev. Benjamin Barnes, he was a local and assistant minister at Barnes Methodist Church for eight years. He helped found, and was one of the first trustees of, Mount Horeb Methodist Church in Southampton County.

Jacob Davis Barnes, born c1820 – He was a Methodist Minister as was his father, Rev. Benjamin Barnes. He migrated to Schuyler County, Missouri.

Mills Burwell Barrett, born 1826 – A Christian Church Minister, he founded Barrett's Christian Church. He served as a Chaplain to the 12th Va. infantry during the Civil War and was killed at Spotsylvania Court House.

Wyatt Smith Woodard, born c1831 – Very little is known of the Reverend Woodard other than cemetery records indicate he was a pastor. He married into the Barham family and seemed to be living in Southampton County in 1856 when his daughter was born.

David Barrow, born c1835 – He was a Baptist Minister of whom little is known. He may have served Black Creek Baptist Church in the northeast of Southampton County.

Nathan Bangs Foushee, born 1848 – He was a Methodist minister who, from 1896 to 1899, served the charge that included Barnes, New Hope, Newsoms, and Mt. Horeb churches.

The original intent of this section of this narrative was to list all the Revolutionary War participants found in this research guide. It was found that the number of veterans would exceed several hundred as there are over 1,500 males in the guide who would have been of an age to serve with the Continental Army. It is unknown about the surrounding counties but, according to Thomas C. Parramore's history of the county, Southampton sent a company of militia (minute men) and a company of regulars to the conflict. There were undoubtedly others who joined the effort from the seven other Southampton County militia companies besides those in these two companies. Captain of the minute men was Henry Taylor who is in this guide. The captain of the regulars was Thomas Ridley, also in this guide. Participation in the surrounding areas was probably similar. The reader of this guide is encouraged to check online the data base of the Daughters of the American Revolution to find their ancestor. This link will take the researcher to the DAR search engine: **https://services.dar.org/Public/DAR_Research/search/**

Much has been said and written about Nat Turner and the Southampton Insurrection. Many authors attempt to interpret the facts to make some point to prove some preconceived notion of what happened and why. Your humble author of this work has read many of those works. (Note: opinion follows) Generally some misguided writer will take some exaggerated, unsubstantiated accounts from some period periodical written and printed many miles from the scene using hear-say information and quote it as fact. To date, the most authoritative, best researched, documented and footnoted is *Nat Turner and the Rising in Southampton County* by David F. Allmendinger, Jr. Some, but certainly not all, of the following has been gleaned from Mr. Allmendinger's book. Mr. Allmendinger has given much genealogical information in his book. This author has tried to find where he (Mr. Allmendinger) might have made an error. This author could find none by Mr. Allmendinger, but he did find some of his own.

On August 22, 1831, Nat Turner and other slaves began a revolt against their white masters. Before they were stopped, they had murdered 55 men, women, and children, including at least 3 infants in their cradles. Of the 55 victims, only 11 were males over the age of 16. Of those 11, only 1 was able to arm and defend himself. Forty-four victims were women and children – 20 women aged 16 or older and 24 children under the age of 16 years. Perhaps some argument in mitigation for the murder of the adult white males in a system of slavery might be made. Maybe, to a lesser degree, the same argument of mitigation may be made in regard to the adult women. But no serious, rational, or intelligent argument can ever be made justifying the murder, or rather the slaughter, with axes and clubs of 24 children, some of whom were infants.

The following are victims of Nat Turner who can be found in this research guide. Names in parentheses are the maiden names of the adult women by which they are listed in the index of this guide. The names are listed in the approximate order in which they were murdered, according to research by Mr. Allmendinger.

Joseph Travis, 30

Sarah (Francis) Moore Travis, 30, wife of Joseph Travis and sister of Salathiel Francis

Putnam Moore, 10, son of Sarah Moore Travis and Thomas Moore, deceased. Putnam Moore was the legal owner of Nat Turner.

Infant Travis, under 1 year old, believed to be a boy. Given name has been lost to time. Infant son of Joseph and Sarah Travis. Not listed in the research guide.

Salathiel Francis, 28

Piety (Vick) Reese, 59

Joseph William H. Reese, 18, son of Piety V. Reese

Elizabeth (Reese) Williamson Turner, 37, wife of Samuel G. Turner. She was killed at the Turner home. Mr. Allmendinger also noted a Sarah Turner, 36, killed at the same time and place as Elizabeth R. Turner. This is probably a sister of Samuel G. Turner although no record has been found to verify this assumption.

Henry Bryant, 25

Elizabeth (Balmer) Bryant, 22, wife of Henry Bryant

Infant Bryant, about 1, sex unknown, child of Henry and Elizabeth Bryant not listed in research guide.

Mildred (unknown) Balmer, 60, mother of Elizabeth B. Bryant

Catherine (Whitehead) Whitehead, 59, Catherine Whitehead married her cousin John Whitehead who died about 1806. The Whiteheads had 12 children, 5 of whom were killed by Nat Turner.

Richard Whitehead, 30, son of Catherine Whitehead

Minerva Whitehead, 25, daughter of Catherine Whitehead

Mary Ann Whitehead, 23, daughter of Catherine Whitehead

Mourning Ann Whitehead, 19, daughter of Catherine Whitehead

Margaret Whitehead, 37, daughter of Catherine Whitehead

In addition to the above Whiteheads, Mr. Allmendinger found evidence of a Whitehead grandson, age 2, killed in the attack but does not speculate of who the child's parents might be. Catherine Whitehead also had a daughter Martha who was married to Jepthah Darden. Their son Jacob kept a Bible in which he recorded births and deaths. In that Bible he listed the death of his younger brother, John Edward Darden, born 13 Nov. 1824, died 22 Aug. 1831. It is possible, maybe even probable, that the Whitehead grandson killed is John Edward Darden aged 6. John Edward Darden is listed in the research guide.

John L.(or W.) Browne, 3

Samuel T. Browne, 7 Both John and Samuel Browne are the orphan sons of Thomas D. and Mary (Polly) Francis Browne. Thomas and Mary both died in 1829 and the boys were taken in by their uncle, Nathaniel Francis, the brother of Mary. Both John and Samuel were murdered at the home of their uncle.

John Thomas Barrow, 26, was the only victim who had time to arm himself.

George Vaughan, 19, was the brother-in-law of John Thomas Barrow and was killed at Barrow's home. He is also a son of Rebecca Foster Vaughan noted below.

Martha (Kindred) Waller, 45, was the wife of Levi Waller who survived. Levi Waller had been married 3 times by 1831. He married Martha Kindred in 1804. Also killed from the Waller household that day was daughter Martha age 4, two sons ages 9 and 7, an infant, and a daughter, 26. In addition there were three 10 year olds murdered who attended school at the Waller home.

Rebecca (Foster) Vaughan, 47 Her home, where she was murdered, has been preserved at the Southampton Agricultural and Forestry Museum.

Ann Eliza Vaughan, 19, daughter of Rebecca F. Vaughan

William Arthur Vaughan 16, son of Rebecca F. Vaughan

In total, 26 of Nat Turner's victims are subjects of this research guide (plus the infants). Hopefully, the reader will come to know that these 26 were living, loving, breathing human beings, not merely some number listed on a page in a musty history book.

The decade of the 1830's ended much as it had begun, with a mass murder. On the night of Monday, December 12, 1840, five people were bludgeoned to death in the home James Jordan (the younger) Scott. Those killed were Scott, his sister Ann Pretlow, her granddaughter Sarah C. Pretlow, a free black servant Lydia Mingo, and her young son Seth Mingo. The information relayed in this tale was gathered from the Southampton County Circuit Court (SCCC) Minute Book (1835-1842), the SCCC Order Book (1839-1843), the Southampton Will Books (WB12&13), and the Southampton Deed Books (DB24 &25), as well as a story printed by The *Portsmouth Times* of 16 December, 1840. Another servant girl managed to escape the slaughter and lived to relate the events.

The servant girl identified Matthew Drake as the murderer. Supposedly, after the murders, Matthew Drake ransacked the house looking for money and then set fire to the home to cover his deeds. Neighbors, alerted by the servant girl that something was amiss, arrived at the house soon thereafter and put out the blaze that had done only minor damage. The robbery motive and the arson attempt have only been found in the *Portsmouth Times* story and was not mentioned in the court records. Drake was arraigned for first degree murder on 21 December 1840, and ordered held without bond.

On 1 April 1841, twenty-four men were summoned to sit as a grand jury. Twenty-one showed up. They returned five indictments for murder. Four were true bills; one was not a true bill. Of the twenty-one grand jurors, fourteen are in this guide: Dr. Cuthbert D. Barham (the foreman), Rev. Simon Murfree, John Moore (Sr.), Edward Crumpler, James E. Crichlow, William Edwards, Mills Pope, George Williams, Davis Barrett, Lewis Worrell, John Thorpe, William B. Pope, Levi Waller, James L Gray, and Byrd Lundy. Two of the three no shows (who would be summoned to court for failure to appear contempt of court charges) are also listed in this guide: Thomas D. Knight and Mills L. Gray.

The next day, 2 April, 1841, Matthew Drake was tried and found guilty. He pleaded not guilty and would remain adamant about his innocence until the end. Of the twelve men who found him guilty, four are in this guide: John Moore (Jr.), Jordan Edwards. John Vick and Benjamin E. Pope.

One week later, 8 April 1841, Matthew Drake appeared in court for sentencing. Before sentence was passed, he was asked if he had anything to say and again he protested his innocence. He was sentenced to be hanged on the 21 May 1841.

James Scott, Ann Pretlow, Sarah Pretlow, and Matthew Drake can all be found in this guide. James Scott, like most of the Scotts in Southampton County, was a Quaker who had manumitted his slaves years ago. Most of the Quaker Scotts had freed their slaves with one notable exception which will be discussed later in this narrative. James Scott, like his parents (James Jordan and Miriam Scott) before him, largely made a living by financing land sales and other items through deeds of trust. The *Portsmouth Times* story stated the motive of the murders was robbery; however, it was never found that anything was stolen. One of the properties upon which James Scott loaned money and took a deed of trust was the 44 acre home of Matthew Drake. That was on 19 October 1829, Deed Book 21, page 207, in the amount of $320.72. This land bordered land owned by Scott. How much Matthew still owed Scott on the debt is not known, but he still owed some and probably was in default as evidenced by the fact that foreclosure proceedings took place after the execution.

Between the time of his sentencing and his execution, Matthew was visited in jail by representatives of the James Jordan Scott estate and the estate of Ann Pretlow. James Jordan Scott had a will by which he willed all he had to his sister Ann. No will for Ann has been found. It seems there was some question as to whom Scott's estate was to go. If Ann had predeceased James Scott, then the estate was to go to other heirs. If James passed away before Ann, then Ann or her heirs were to receive the estate. The representatives of the two estates were hoping Matthew could tell them which he had killed first, or to be more specific, who died first: James or Ann. Matthew, as he had throughout the ordeal, stated his innocence so he had no idea who had first succumbed.

The *Portsmouth Times* story stated that over $15,000 in silver had been found in Scott's home after his death. The estate inventories listed no such amount, in fact, nowhere close to that amount. There might not have been $15,000 in silver coin in the entire county in 1840. However, the inventory of Ann's estate listed more than $16,000 in promissory notes and deeds of trust that had been transferred from the estate of her brother. Evidently, the lawyers figured the estates out.

The Order Book of 21 Jun 1841, ordered that the estate of Matthew Drake be committed to Sheriff Thomas Pretlow for administration according to law. On 5 June 1848, a deed was recorded by Jesse Drewry, substitute trustee appointed by the court, for the land formally belonging to Matthew Drake who was in default of a deed of trust (Deed Book 26, page 348). The land was sold at public auction. The high bidder was Mariah Joyner Drake, widow of Matthew. Her high bid, with 12 months credit, was $85 for 44 acres with a house to which she now had free and clear title. It is strongly suspected that no one bid against her and what she paid was far below what was owed (remember the original note was for $320.72).

The Murfreesboro Historical Association has done an absolutely wonderful job promoting the preservation of historic buildings and sites within the town and restoring some of the older buildings there. The Association's tours have no less than 52 sites for one to see. Their *Candlelight Christmas Tour* early in the yuletide season rivals anything one might see in Colonial Williamsburg. Historic Murfreesboro is very much like Colonial Williamsburg except placed one to three generations later in time. Several of the preserved buildings have direct connections to several people within this guide.

Roberts-Vaughan Village Center – 116 East Main Street: Once was owned by Uriah Vaughan. Uriah was born c1813 and was the son of John Vaughan and Sarah Rogers.

The Murfree-Williams House -318 Williams Street: Was once, about 1793, a school run by the Reverend Joseph Gurley (bc1746) prior his moving to Tennessee and after his time as minister of St. Luke's Church in what today is Courtland, the county seat of neighboring Southampton County. Joseph Gurley had replaced his father, Rev. George Gurley (II), as the minister of St. Luke and his younger brother, the Rev. George Gurley (III),was minister at Barnes Methodist 12 miles and just across the state line from Murfreesboro.

Pipkin-Harrell-Chitty House – 207 North Wynn Street: Built by Dr. Isaac Pipkin c1792, the son of John Pipkin whose father was also an Isaac Pipkin. The Association states that at one time the house was home to part of the Chitty family but it does not state which ones. All the early Chittys are listed in this guide.

D. A. Barnes House – 625 West Main Street: This house was built about 1874 by David Anderson Barnes, born 1834, the son of Cullin William Barnes of Northampton County, NC.

As wonderful as this preserved area is, there is a problem of perception. The same problem exists in Colonial Williamsburg but to an even greater extent. Most people today do not understand that the thin slice of life presented by the Murfreesboro Historical Society and Colonial Williamsburg did not exist beyond the town limits of Murfreesboro or beyond Duke of Gloucester Street in Williamsburg. The people represented are the elite of local society; doctors, lawyers, judges, merchants, while the vast majority of people lived on farms scratching out a living from the earth in a world that is not represented often today by any exhibits or museums.

After disastrous crop years in 1814 and 1815, Peter Blow had had enough of farm life in Southampton County, Virginia. So he packed up his 6 children (three more would be born later), wife, and slaves, including one he called Sam Blow, and moved to Huntsville, Alabama, where he was sure the farming would be better. It was not. So in1823, he moved the family to St. Louis to open and run a boarding house and rented out Sam and his other slaves.

Although documentation is sketchy at best, it would seem Sam was born on Peter Blow's grandfather's plantation about 1799. John Scott's daughter, Mary, had married Richard Blow. These were the parents of Peter Blow. Sam had passed from John Scott, to his daughter Mary Scott Blow, to her son Peter. Peter Blow died in 1832 and Sam was to be sold. At that time, Sam made known he wished to be called by the name he was given at his birth on John Scott's plantation – Etheldred Scott. Etheldred is not in this guide but all the others named are, including all nine of Peter Blow's children.

Etheldred Scott was sold to an army surgeon by the name of John Emerson who took Etheldred to military posts in "free" states and territories for several years. Because he had lived in those free states, Etheldred sued for his freedom. He lost, but Peter Blow's son, Peter Etheldred Blow, purchased Etheldred Scott's freedom. To history, Etheldred is known as Dred Scott.

One of the basic tenets of this guide is to concentrate on people born prior to 1850 and the advent of the first really comprehensive census. What follows is the last portion of this narrative. It deals with an aspect of the War Between the States and, while the war itself dates after 1850, all those who participated in it were born prior to that year. No Union soldiers are listed. This fact is not due to any bias, but rather due to the fact there were no sources available. Surely some of those who migrated to other parts of the country or their offspring must have fought for the Union, but such information was unavailable within the scope of this research guide.

There is one notable exception. Major General George Henry Thomas had a distinguished career during the war, rising to command an army. Legend has it that Thomas remained loyal to the Union in exchange for a promise that the Union would refrain from operations within Southampton County, Virginia. This is probably not true. What is true is that his sisters turned his portrait to face the wall, never to turn it back as long as they lived. During the hard times of reconstruction, Thomas sent money to help his sisters. They refused to cash the checks. When George Henry Thomas died, none of his Southampton relatives attended the funeral.

When Baby-Boomers encountered some male of their father's age and their curiosity was aroused, the question was not "Were you in the war?" but rather "What did you do in the war?" of course meaning WWII. It was just assumed that all were in the war, and for the most part, all were. The war was an all-out effort.

For the South during the War Between the States, it was even more of an all-out effort that comes with a sense of urgency of having one's home invaded. According to history.answers.com, over 90% of the men of an age to fight were in the Confederate service.

This research guide lists approximately 900 men born between the years 1820 to 1846. If 90% of those listed served for the South, the total would be more than 800 Confederate veterans. Obviously, this is more people than can be listed in this narrative. But as this is being written, the day happens to be Memorial Day; therefore, it is only fitting that those listed in this guide who lost their lives in that conflict be remembered.

Davis P. Bryant: died 1 Aug. 1862 in camp of measles, age 29

Collin Edwards: 3rd Va. Infantry, died 1862 of disease, age 37

Benjamin Whitley: 1st NC Infantry, killed at Ellyson's Mill, 1862, age 17

George W. Gurley: 3rd Va. Infantry, killed at Frazier's Farm (Glendale), 1862, age 22

George H. Gurley: killed at Gaines Mill, 27 June 1862, age 18

Benjamin C. Brett: 3rd Va. Infantry, killed at Frazier's Farm, 30 June 1862, age 20

Edward Lewis Everett: 3rd Va. Infantry, died of disease, 30 June 1862, age 17 (although the sources say Edward died of disease, note he died on the day his unit was engaged at Frazier's Farm)

Robert T. Gray: 3rd Va. Infantry, killed at Frazier's Farm, 30 June 1862, age 25

Lloyd W. Drake: 9th Va. Infantry, killed at Malvern Hill, 1 July 1862, age 36

Nathan A. Jones: 41st Va. Infantry, wounded at Malvern Hill, 1 July 1862, died 28 Aug., age 25

Joseph H. Ellsworth: 41st Va. Infantry, died in Richmond, 10 September, 1862, age 30

John W. E. Bishop: 5th Va. Calvary, died of disease, October, 1862, age 24

John T. Bryant: 3rd Va. Infantry, died of wounds, 8 October 1862, age 28

Eldridge N. Williams: 18th Va. Artillery, killed at Winchester, Va., 1 November 1862, age 18

John N. Barrett: 3rd Va. Infantry, killed at Winchester, Va., November, 1862, age 23

Benjamin J. Barrett: 3rd Va. Infantry, died of disease, 11 November 1862, age 39

Mills H. Bryant: 41st Va. Infantry, died in Lynchburg of typhoid, 23 November 1862, age 18

John Tomlin: died in Richmond, 25 November 1862, age 31

Lewis W. Barrett: 3rd Va. Infantry, killed in action, 1863, age 20

John L. Beale: 41st Va. Infantry, killed 1863, age 33

Joseph T. Ferguson: 3rd Va. Infantry, died of wounds in Point Lookout Prison, Md., 1863, age 20

Collin Kitchen, Jr.: 9th Va. Infantry, killed 1863, age 21

Joseph Henry Worrell: 3rd Va. Infantry, died in Point Lookout Prison, Md., 1863, age 25

Owen Drake: killed 1863, age 26

James W. Joyner: 18th Va. Artillery, died of disease, 11 Jan. 1863, age 28

Benjamin L Barnes: 13th Va. Calvary, died "medical", 25 January 1863, age 21

Benjamin Barnes: 18th Va. Artillery, died of disease, 26 January. 1863, age 24

Jordan Beale: 41st Va. Infantry, died of wounds in battle, 27 February, 1863, age 17

Everett E. Griffin: 41st Va. Infantry, wounded 17 Aug. 1862 Sharpsburg, Md., died 20 May 1863 in Richmond, age 26

Jesse W. Worrell: killed July 9, 1863, age 19

Thomas Everett, Jr.: 3rd Va. Infantry, killed 3 July 1863 at Gettysburg, Penn., age 18

Richard B. L. Everett: 3rd Va. Infantry, killed at Gettysburg 3 July 1863, age 28

Norman W. Beale: 13th Va. Calvary, wounded at Gettysburg, died Williamsport, Md., 8 July 1863, age 27

Joseph W. Pope: 3rd Va. Infantry, wounded at Gettysburg, died 11 July 1863, age 25

Joseph Ezra Gillette: 13th Va. Calvary, killed Brandy Station, Va., 1 November 1863, age 36

Henry Whitley: 1st NC Infantry, died of wounds received at Gettysburg, Nov. 1863, age 20

John W. Chitty: 9th Va. Infantry, died of disease, 3 November 1863, age 20

William C. Chitty: 3rd Va. Infantry, captured 1864, died in prison 1865, age 27

John Whitehead Darden: 3rd Va. Infantry, died of disease, 19 October 1863, age 29

John T. Griffin: 41st Va. Infantry, killed at Spotsylvania Court House, 8 May 1864, age 21

Richard B. Ferguson: 41st Va. Infantry, Wounded Spotsylvania C. H., died 2 Sept. 1864, age 24

Robert J. Velvin: 41st Va. Infantry, killed, 5 September 1864, age 34

John Fletcher Beale: 13th Va. Calvary, killed at Hicksford (Emporia) Va., 28 Dec. 1864, age 22

Mills Burwell Barrett: 12th Va. Infantry, Chaplin, wounded Spotsylvania C. H., died 1865, age 38

John Darius Brett: killed at the Battle of New Market, 1865, age 42

Calvin D. Cutler: 3rd Va. Infantry, killed at Five Forks, Dinwiddie County, 3 April 1865, age 22

Ashbury W. Cobb: 13th Va. Calvary, killed on the retreat to Appomattox, 5 April 1865, age 21

In addition, there are 9 other young men in this guide who, in their early twenties, died during the period 1861 to 1865. No information is available as to any Confederate service, although it is suspected they did serve and die during the conflict.

Today when we watch some TV show or movie depicting the Civil War Soldier, it is easy to get the impression the war was fought by middle-aged men. The movie "Gettysburg" is a good example. This movie, like many others, made extensive use of Civil War re-enactors. Re-enactors tend to be middle- to late middle-aged individuals (men who have raised their families and now have the time to participate in re-enactments) and it shows in the aged faces. The sad truth is the Civil War, like all wars, was fought by young men. The forty-seven men listed above have an average age of 25.7 years. Seventeen year olds outnumber men in their 40's. Eighteen and nineteen year olds outnumber men in their 30's.

EPILOG: When George Washington crossed the Delaware River on Christmas night, 1776, he stood in the bow of the boat. He did not help row. Everybody remembers that. No one remembers who did row the boat.

It is said that Union General U.S. Grant first faced Confederate General R. E. Lee on May 5, 1864, at the Wilderness of Spotsylvania County, Virginia. They did not face each other, but nearly a couple hundred thousand of their soldiers did. When Lee and Grant finally did meet face to face, it was April 9, 1865, at Appomattox. By that time, over one hundred thousand men had been killed, were missing, or had been wounded since the 5th of May in Virginia.

All of us, both past and present, make a contribution to history. For the vast majority of us, it is a very, very minute contribution which, if removed, would make absolutely no difference to the general history. Two or three of us removed – same thing. But, if the contributions of enough of us were to be removed, Washington would still be on the Pennsylvania shore of the Delaware River gazing over at New Jersey. Lee and Grant would be lost in the thickets of the Wilderness.

Family history –and by extension genealogy- is history on the "atomic" level. Like the atom is to matter, family history is the basic building block upon which all history is based. For this reason, family history is important. All history begins with people, not places or dates. Places and dates derive their historical importance from human activity (people doing things). And family is the basic human activity.

Research note: In his history of Southampton County, Virginia, Thomas Parramore states that Dred Scott "was born near Edom, in the Shenandoah Valley, in 1809." Parramore gives as his source *The Dred Scott Decision* by Charles Morrow Wilson. Britannica.com, Wikipedia, and several other reference sites, however, all state Scott to have been born in Southampton. Edom is in the northwest section of Rockingham County. The location is actually closer to West Virginia than it is to the county seat of Harrisonburg. According to Google Maps, by today's roads the distance between Edom and the Blow plantation in Southampton is about 220 miles. It would probably take a rider on horseback 7 to 8 days to cover that distance circa 1810 – a wagon or mule cart about 10 to 14 days (given the mountains and hills that would have to have been traversed. These estimates are probably conservative.) The cost to transport a slave child from Edom to Southampton would probably exceed the market value of the child. While it may be possible that Dred Scott was transported as a child from Edom to Southampton, it is not probable that such happened.

Final Thoughts

&

Errata

From a philosophical point of view, no genealogical work is ever finished, nor can it be. At some point the researcher reaches the end of the paper trail but he never reaches the end - or rather the beginning - of his family. At least he can perceive it to be the end of the paper trail, but there is always the possibility of some obscure record being found in some place where no one has thought to look.

The challenge is, after a given amount of research is done, what ultimately does one do with the information? For most of us, it just sits on a shelf or in a closet gathering dust until we either pass it on to someone who will appreciate it or we die and our heirs have to decide to continue the work, throw it all away, or stick it in their closet to gather a new crop of dust. One cannot help but speculate how often good information was tossed in the trash, and we can only hope that some future researcher will (or has) re-discovered it.

Some researchers will try to publish. Some will transfer their research to a library, historical society, or genealogical society. If they publish, they have to decide what content to include and establish a point where their work will begin and end. At that point, or some point thereafter, they will find out how immune to criticism they are and how well they did their research. It is a given that someone will question the work. It is invariable that new records and sources will turn up after the work is published that the researcher did not find. This will happen. A good example of this can be found in the narrative *Respectful Disagreement.* The only question is how polite and kind - or impolite and mean - the revealers of the new information will be toward the publishing researcher. There will always be others who feel the published work challenges their genealogical beliefs and tenets and they will be resentful. It happens.

Researchers who donate their research to local libraries, historical, or genealogical societies need to be aware their research might not stay intact. Those collections of families usually take the form of loose-leaf notebooks, composition books, and loose papers in folders. The author of this work has been to several libraries and read the contributions of others given in the above forms only to return at a later date to find some or much of the information missing, pages torn from composition books, and sheets gone from the notebooks and files. The purloined information was taken by some person who did not have the foresight to bring a paper and pen with which to take notes or they found the information offended their previously held notions and research and they appoint themselves censors of a work they deemed offensive. Either way, the collection is damaged or the information lost unless backup sheets exist. Destroying someone else's work because you may disagree with their research and conclusions is extremely narrow-minded.

For the conscientious researcher, the researcher who tries to properly document his findings with sources, the most insidious places to display his work are the online family trees and the sites that allow anyone to edit their work. Many of these sites do not allow for proper documentation and few things can be more disheartening than having well-documented work changed by another because their Great Auntie Ann said their ancestor was "one of three brothers who came from the old country with a royal land grant because they were the illegitimate sons of the king". (Sooner or later all researchers will encounter all or part of the three brothers legend.) People just do not like having their preconceptions questioned.

When it comes to preconceptions, some of the most stubborn to having our notions altered are we genealogical researchers. We somehow find a way to refute the irrefutable. When the original Virginia shires, or counties, were established in the early 1600's, the lines between the shires to the south of the James River were straight lines that ran from the river to what was to become North Carolina in a southwesterly direction. When the line dividing Nansemond and Isle of Wight crossed the Blackwater River, it created a "corner" of land which was difficult to administer for Nansemond because of the river. This area of under 15 square miles or about 9,500 acres was ceded to Southampton to administer in 1786. After that, some deeds in the affected areas would refer to the "old county line." The author of this work found just how inarticulate he was when he was unable to explain, via Email, to another researcher that the wording in a certain deed referred to the old Nansemond line ("the old county line") and not a redrawn state line between Virginia and North Carolina. The researcher would not consider any possibility that was different from her preconception. The idea that county lines would change was inconceivable, but she could accept that state lines could change (which did happen). This particular farm happened to be one the author and his brother rented for agricultural purposes and was well known to be a bit over a mile from the state line.

Paul Drake, JD, God rest his soul, passed away in 2011 and we lost a true gentleman and an unparalleled author in the world of genealogy. If you ever had the privilege to communicate via Email or in person, or if you had attended one of his workshops, you would have learned Paul was insistent that we not judge the people we researched. As genealogical researchers today, we have no way of knowing what our subjects felt, their emotions, their intelligence, or the pressures of everyday life they may have experienced. In short, as the old saying goes, we can't walk a mile in their shoes, so we have no right to judge the actions, or lack thereof, they may have taken. But it can be safely assumed they did the best they could with the circumstances they encountered.

One cannot help but think that Paul would be appalled by today's trend toward revisionist history in which some insist on applying 21st century morals and standards to 17th, 18th, and 19th century people. They, the people of the earlier centuries, are condemned for not thinking as we do today or acting as we would today although their thoughts and actions that are being condemned today were well within the accepted social standards and norms of their eras. Not only is this unfair to those who have come before us, but it exhibits a level of willful ignorance as to what those they criticize faced in their time. It is manifestly unfair and cowardly to criticize those who cannot defend themselves or their actions.

Your humble author is convinced that our ancestors of the 17th thru 20th centuries would fare better in our world of today than we would in their world of yesterday. This is due to our ignorance of their ways and this leads to misconceptions. An example: some years back, a lady researcher could not understand why an ancestor and another man were given only a small fine for "chopping the ears" of another man's hogs. Surely such an act of animal cruelty should have resulted in jail time. In short she thought the ancestor must have been a truly horrid person. (As I recall, the case was from the Southampton County Court Minute Book of 1750 and involved one of the many John Drakes.) It is not known if this John Drake was a truly horrid person or not, but he was not guilty of animal cruelty. Hogs are not branded but, because they are almost impossible to keep in a split rail fence that they "root" under with ease, a method had to be used to identify one's swine. Generally the method used was to notch (chop) the ears of the hog. A notch, or two or three, in the ear of a hog in a certain place on one ear or the other would mark the hog as belonging to a specific person. (My father would notch the ears of pigs he wanted to keep as breeding stock so they would not be accidently taken to market.) The John Drake and his cohort may have been guilty of attempted petty theft of a pig by changing the notch (chopping the ear), but not of animal cruelty. But the lady researcher, being a city girl, would have no reason to know this; however poor John gets misaligned in the process.

Up until 1875 Virginia had a dual court system. There was a court of law where decisions were based on the law and there was the chancery court or court of equity where decisions were based on what was fair. Chancery courts began in old England where a person or group would petition the King for redress of some problem that they felt the law could not properly address. The King would generally hand the petition to his Chancellor to adjudicate. The Chancellor would then hold a hearing, or court, to hear arguments on the petition and then render his decision in the name of the King. The reason this is brought up is because, until 1875, most cases involving wills or family squabbles were heard in chancery court and that is where one can find piles of genealogical information. Not only are the relationships between the parties given, but also where the parties resided. In genealogy, the chancery records are often an underutilized resource. Today only the court of law exists. That court will decide what is legal but not necessarily what is fair – sometimes a shame.

People who use this research guide and find their ancestor need to be aware that their heritage is English – not British. There was not a Great Britain prior to 1707, at which time Queen Anne bribed the Scottish Parliament into voting for the Unification. Most all of the early settlers of Isle of Wight/Southampton had been here for years by then.

Two years, three months, and seven days: That is how much time was required to print family sheets and index the 13,233 people that can be found in this research guide. This figure includes the people for whom their given names were known but not their surnames, and vice versa. All this printing and indexing was part-time work. During planting or harvesting time, two or three weeks might have passed when no work at all was done on the project.

Having reviewed each and every one of those 13,233 people, the author of this research guide is convinced that some are probably duplicated. Instead of six John Does, the estimated birth years are probably off and there may be only four or five of the lads. Rather than John who married a Jane and John who married a Joan, it is possible there was but one John married twice to both Jane and Joan but no record was found to confirm this - yet.

In reviewing the estimated birth years, it is thought that the years given are generally within 4 years of the actual birth year over half the time – about 54-58%. Birth year estimates are from 5 to 10 years off, about 30-35% of the time. If there are big differences in the estimated birth years, the actual it is generally thought to be in the large families where there might be 20 or more years between the youngest and oldest siblings. This might occur only a very small percentage of the time, but it could lead to the same person being listed as two people as the estimated ages would seem to be nearly a generation apart.

There are more than 110 people included in this research guide who were in Isle of Wight, Virginia, in 1658, over three hundred and fifty years ago. There were 208 surnames or maybe a bit more in the new county when Southampton was formed from Isle of Wight in 1749, more than two hundred and fifty years ago. In this research guide an accumulated 10,000 or so people have been identified as living prior to 1850, over 150 years ago. But what the author of this work would dearly love to know and does not know is how to find out or estimate how many people <u>today</u> can trace their genealogical heritage back to the Southampton/Isle of Wight area? And what would be the total number of people through the years who can call the area their ancestral home?

Errata

Errata are defined (yeah, it sounds funny to me too, but Errata is the plural of Erratum so are it is and is it isn't) as a list of errors in printing or writing. When the family sheets were saved, they had to be saved in a "Rich Text Format" to a "Word" program. The two are not completely compatible. Most of the errors were in Spacing or line placement, not all of which the author is computer savvy enough to correct – ergo the errata is far too great to list. The author begs for the reader's forgiveness and indulgence.

Bibliography

Allmendinger, David F., *Nat Turner and the Rising in Southampton County,* Johns Hopkins University Press, 2014

Beatty, John D. and Vick, Di An, editors, , *Joseph Vick of Lower Parish, Isle of Wight County, Virginia and his Descendants, Vol. 1.*, Genus Publishing, 2004

Boddie, John B., *Seventeenth Century Isle of Wight County, Virginia*, currently published by Heritage Books, (1938), 2007

Brody, Jane Drake, "Richard Drake of Southampton – Va.", Family Report

Chandler, Betty Barrett and Askew, Malita Rawls, "Barrett Family"

Chapman, Blanche Adams, *Wills and Administrations of Isle of Wight County, Virginia 1647-1800,* currently published by Heritage Books, (1938), 2006

Chapman, Blanche Adams, *Wills and Administrations of Southampton County, Virginia, 1749-1800,* currently published by Heritage Books, 1998, 2008

Commonwealth of Virginia
- Division of Vital Statistics
- Isle of Wight County, Deeds
- Isle of Wight County, Great Book
- Southampton County, Court Records
- Southampton County, Death Record
- Southampton County, Deed Books
- Southampton County, Guardian Accounts 1776-1810
- Southampton County, Land Tax Books 1782-1849
- Southampton County, Marriage Register 1749-1850
- Southampton County, Tax List Personal Property
- Southampton County, Will Books
- Surry County, Court Records, Order Book
- Surry County, Wills
- Sussex County, Court Records

Council, Judson, *Hodges Council of Virginia, and Descendants,* J. H. Furst Co., 1941

Davis, Eliza Timberlake, *Surry County, Wills and Administrations,* currently published by Heritage Books, (1955, 1980) 2007

Dorman, John Frederick, *Adventures of Purse and Person,* currently published by Heritage Books, (2004) 2012

Drake, Charles E. F., "Origins of the Drake Family of Isle of Wight, Virginia", National Genealogical Society Quarterly

Drake, Charles E. F., *The Drake Family of Washington County, Georgia,* Gateway Press, 2005

Drake, Paul, *Now in Our Fourth Century,* Heritage Books, 1999

Drewry, William Sidney, *The Southampton Insurrection,* The Neal Company, 1900

Edwards, Bruce M., "The Edwards Family of Northampton", 1975

Greer, George Cabel, *Early Virginia Immigrants,* currently published by Heritage Books, (1912) 2018
Transcriptions compiled by Allen Price, 2011, www.EVMEDIA.com/Virginia

Grimes, J. Bryan, *North Carolina Wills and Inventories,* Clearfield Company, 1912, 2005

Hart, Lyndon and Nichol, Bromfield, *Ridley of Southampton,* B. B. Nichol, 1992

Hinshaw, William Wade, *Encyclopedia of American Quaker Genealogy,* publisher unknown, 1936, 1950

Hotton, John C., *Originial List of Persons of Quality, 1600-1700,* currently published by Heritage Books, (1874) 2007

Joyner, Ulysses P., Jr., *Joyner of Southampton,* McClure Printing Company, 1975

Morton, Oren Frederic, *History of Pendleton County, West Virginia,* Regional Publishing Co., 1910, 1974

North Carolina
- Bertie County, Court Records
- Bertie County, Wills
- Gates County, Court Records
- Halifax County, Wills
- Hertford County, Court Records
- Hertford County, Deeds
- Hertford County, Marriage Records
- Hertford County, Wills
- Northampton County, Deeds and Wills
- Northampton County, Marriage Register
- State Archives, will posted on line

Parramore, Thomas C., *Southampton County Virginia,* University Press of Virginia, 1978

Sanders, Bruce, "Southampton Cemetery Project", www.SouthamptonHistory.org

South Petherton Parish, "Baptismal Register", as researched by Charles E. F. Drake

Tidewater News, Franklin Virginia, Newspaper, Various Obituaries

United States of America
- 1830 Census
  - Southampton County, Virginia
- 1850 Census
  - Hertford County, North Carolina
  - Southampton County, Virginia
- 1860 Census
  - Southampton County, Virginia
- 1870 Census
  - Southampton County, Virginia
- 1880 Census
  - Southampton County, Virginia

1900 Census
Southampton County, Virginia

Virtual Jamestown web-site, “Indentured Servants Data Base”, date on-going, www.virtualjamestown.org

Warren County (Ohio) Historical Society, www.wchsmuseum.org

William and Mary Quarterly (The College of), various articles quoted

Winborne, Benjamin B., Judge, *Vaughan Family of Hertford County,* 1909

Index

Aggie; 12
Ahoskie; 95
Albemarle Sound, 97
Anglican; 87, 98
Ann, Queen; 110
Alcohol Taxation; 40
Allen; 5
  Arthur; 97
  Wright; 12
Allin (see Allen); 5
Allmendinger
  David; 100
Allon (see Allen); 5
America; 79, 98
Anderson; 5
Andersen (see Anderson); 5
Angus; 71
Applewhite; 5
Applewait (see Applewhite); 5
Appomattox (Va.); 39, 71, 107
Argonne Forest; 74
Armistead
  Louis; 39
Army; 76
Artis
  George; 79, 80
Atkinson
  Amos; 65
  Elizabeth; 65

Baby-Boomers; 105
Bacon
  Nathanial; 96, 97
Bacon's
  Castle; 68, 97
  Rebellion; 4
Bailey; 5
  Rebecca; 90
Balmer
  Elizabeth; 101
  Mildred; 101
Baptist; 36, 40, 100
Barbeque Swamp; 88
Barham
  Cuthbert; 102
Barnes; 27
  Benjamin; 27-32, 35, 36, 43-47, 49, 50, 85, 99, 100, 106
  Burwell; 32, 44
  Catherine Simmons; 32
  Cullin; 104
  David A.; 104
  Dorothy; 50, 64, 85
  Edward; 28, 43, 96
  Elizabeth; 44, 46, 47.50
  Family; 2
  Jacob; 27-32, 35, 36, 43-47, 49, 50, 64, 84, 100
  James; 29, 30, 43-45, 47, 49, 50
  John; 31, 46, 89, 91
  Josiah; 28, 29, 43-47, 50, 52
  Joshua; 28, 29, 44, 45, 47, 49, 50
  Levenia; 43-47, 50
  Linney; 43-45, 50
  Marmaduke; 31, 46
Barnes (cont.)
  Martha; 31, 43, 44, 46
  Matilda Worrell; 46
  Mary; 31, 44, 46
  Methodist Church; 21, 27, 28, 31-40, 45, 46, 49, 60, 74, 85, 98, 99, 100, 104
  Nancy Ann; 29, 31, 32, 43-45, 49, 50
  Patience Oliver; 52
  Priscilla; 44, 47
  Richard; 31, 46
  Robert; 31, 32, 46, 49, 50, 85, 99
  Sally; 47
  Samuel; 29, 47
  Sarah; 29, 45, 47, 50
  Sela; 29, 44, 45, 47, 50
  Simmons; 32
  Stephen; 80
  Susan; 49
  Suzannah Oliver; 52
  Thomas; 29, 43-47, 50, 64, 79, 80, 81, 84, 85
  William; 29, 43-50, 52
Barnum
  Dot
Barrett
  Ann; 33
  Benjamin; 27, 32, 36, 46, 49, 105
  Burwell; 33
  Charity; 52
  Davis; 102
  Edmond; 32, 44, 52
  Giles; 33
  Henry; 48
  Jacob; 46
  James; 32
  Jane; 32
  Jesse; 44
  John; 33, 105
  Jordan; 46
  Julia; 48
  Lewis; 106
  Lucy; 30, 32, 33, 45, 46, 49
  Lydia; 33
  Martha; 48
  Mills; 100, 106
  Richard; 48
Barrett Christian Church; 100
Barrett's Chapel; 90
Barrow; 5
  David; 100
  John; 96, 102
  Joseph; 66
Barrows (see Barrow); 5
Basden; 88
Battle
  Ann; 65
  Beach; 65
  Charity; 65
  Isaac; 65
  Joel; 65
  William; 65
Baylie (see Bailey); 5
Beal (see Beale); 5
Beale; 5
  Drury; 80

Beale (cont.)
    Edwin; 63
    John; 63, 106
    Jordan; 106
    Lydia; 47
    Mark Luke; 20
    Norman; 106
Bedford(Va.)
    Circuit; 30
Beel (see Beale); 5
Bennett
    Merchant; 4
    Richard, Gov.; 87
Bentonville, N.C.; 8
Berkley
    William, Gov.; 96, 97
Best
    Peggy; 90
Bethel Road; 67
Bishop
    James; 62
    John; 105
Black Creek; 87
Black Creek Baptist Church; 100
Blackwater River; 4, 10, 67, 87, 88, 110
Blacksmith; 57, 58
Bloomington (Ill); 88
Blont (see Blount); 5
Blount; 5
Blow
    Mary Scott; 104
    Peter; 104
    Richard;104
    Sam; 104
Blunt (see Blount); 5
Bly (see Blythe); 5
Blythe; 5
    John; 91
    Zachariah; 61
Boddie; 5, 87, 88
Body (see Boddie); 5
Bodye (see Boddie); 5
Boon; 5
Boon Bridge Road; 35
Boone (see Boon); 5
Booth; 5
Boothe (see Booth); 5
Bootleg(ing); 15
Borrow (see Barrow); 5
Bottom
    John; 44
Bowels (see Bowles); 5
Bowin
    John; 88, 89
Bowles; 5
Boykins (Va.); 73, 85
Bracewell (see Braswell);5
    Robert; 98
Bracy (see Bressie); 5
Bradley
    William; 64, 82
    Joseph; 89
    Thomas; 89
Branch
    John; 88
Brandy; 7, 8, 39
Brandy Station (Va.); 106
Brantley
    Association; 8
    Ken; 8
Brasey (see Bressie); 5
Braswell; 5
    Richard; 98
Brat (see Brett); 5
Breat (see Brett); 5
Breet (see Brett); 5
Bressie; 5
    Suzanna; 57
Brett (Britt); 27
    Benjamin; 57, 58, 105
    Charity; 56, 57
    Cherry; 34, 55
    Edward, 34, 56, 58
    Elizabeth; 34, 55
    Emmy; 34
    Family; 2, 4, 5, 9
    Henan; 55
    Jesse; 33, 34, 46, 47
    John; 34, 46, 55-58, 107
    Joseph; 57
    Mary Liles; 55
    Missouri; 55
    Nancy; 55
    Nathan; 33, 34, 36, 46, 55-58
    Rebecca; 55
    Rhoda; 34, 56
    Susan McLaughlin; 55
    Suzanna Bressie; 57, 58
    Thomas; 57, 58
    William; 34, 55, 57
Brian (see Bryant); 5
Briand (see Bryant); 5
Briggs
    William; 59
Brisco (Brister); 62
Bristol, England; 69
Britannica.com; 107
British; 110
Britt (see Brett); 4, 5, 27
    Levenia; 45, 46
    Nathan; 27
Broadway (Va); 75
Brock
    James; 61
Brown (see Browne); 5
Browne; 5
    Abraham; 12
    John; 102
    Mary; 65, 81, 82, 102
    Polly; 85, 86
    Samuel; 102
    Samuel, Dr.; 63-65, 81, 82
    Thomas; 102
Brunswick(Va.)
    Circuit; 30
Bryan (see Bryant); 5

Bryant
Davis; 39, 40, 99, 105
Elizabeth; 89, 101
Family; 2
Henry; 101
Joe S.; 8
John; 105
Lewis; 89
Lydia Barrett; 39, 40
Mills; 105
Orman; 39
Richard; 39
Toolly; 39, 40
William, Jr.;39
Buckhorn; 28
Bunker Oil; 76
Burges (see Burgesss); 5
Burgess; 5
Caroline; 85
Henry; 98
Thomas; 98
Burgesses, House of; 96, 97
Burras
Ann; 96
Burrow; 5
John; 96
Burt
Hayley; 50
Bushehr, Iran; 76
Bynum; 5
Drury; 32
Byrum (see Bynum); 5

Cabin Branch; 88
Caesar; 41
Campion (see Champion);5
Candle Light Tour; 103
Capron
Virginia; 28, 85
Carolinas; 96
Caroon; 5
Caroone (see Caroon); 5
Carter
Thomas; 97
Champion; 5
Chancery; 27, 28, 45, 46, 62, 63, 110
Chaplin; 100
Charles I, King; 97
Charles II, King; 68, 96, 97
Chesapeake Bay; 95
Chittee (see Chitty); 5
Chitty; 5
John; 106
William; 71, 106
Christmas; 107
Church of England; 3
Ministers; 98
Church Warden; 87
Circuit Riders; 98, 99
Civil War; 7, 12, 39, 40, 107
Coast Guard; 76
Coggins; 5
Coggin (see Coggins); 5
Cogin (see Coggins); 5
Cocke (see Cook); 5
Richard; 87
Cold Harbor, Va.; 8, 39
Colt Police Positive Special; 20
Colonial Williamsburg; 103, 104
Cobb
Ashbury; 107
Cook; 5
Cooke (see Cook); 5
Cooper
Justinian; 12
Confederate; 105, 107
Congress; 40, 76
Continental Army; 100
Cornwallis; 66
Courtland
Virginia; 5, 28, 67, 104
Cowan; 4, 5
Joseph; 71, 72
Cowand (see Cowan); 4, 5
Cowwins (see Cowan); 4, 5
Crichlow
James; 102
Crumpler
Edward; 102
Cutler
Calvin; 107
Cypress Bridge; 81
Cypress Swamp
The Great; 15, 29, 40, 71
Road; 19, 35

D.A. Barnes House; 104
Darden
Jacob; 101
Jepthah; 101
John; 101
Darden Mill run; 29
Daughters of the American Revolution; 100
Daughtry
Ann; 60
Mary; 60
William; 62
Davis
Arthur; 50
John; 44, 97
Dawel (see Doyal); 5
Delaware River;107
Delaware, Va.; 7
Democrat Party; 16
Denson
Christian; 90, 91
Jordan; 90
Joseph; 90, 91
Martha; 90
Depression; 15
Devon, England; 68
Dinwiddie County; 107
Doctor's Branch; 88
Dorby; 10
Doyal; 5
Doyel (see Doyal); 5

Doyell (see Doyal); 5
Doyle (see Doyal); 5
Drake
Allen; 73
Ann; 67, 68, 81-83
Ann Ellis; 47, 63, 64
Ann Griffin; 67
Arnold; 69
Aaron; 69
Barnaby; 68, 91
Benjamin; 91
Betty; 8
Caroline Sumner; 60
Celia; 67
Charles E. F.; 1, 65, 81
Claude; 29
Conrad; 59
David; 67
Dorothy; 45, 47, 63, 64, 81-83, 85
Drewry; 47, 63, 64, 79-83
Drury; 67, 79, 81, 91
Edna Dorothy Hartman; 21, 22, 74
Elizabeth; 60-65, 67, 81, 82, 91
Emma; 59,60
Ester; 68
Ethelburt; 99
Etheldred; 91
Family; 2, 9
Francis, Sir; 2
George; 13
Grandmamma Edna; 16
Henry; 80
Hines; 64, 67
Honor; 66
Isaac; 66
James; 50, 85, 86, 91
James Thomas; 15, 21
Jemima Parnell; 68
Jeremiah; 60-65, 81-83
Jesse; 47, 60-65, 67, 80-82
Joe H., 6, 27, 43, 45, 55, 59
Joel; 66, 98
John; 13, 59-69, 81, 82, 97, 110
Jonas; 66
Jordan; 66, 98
Joshua; 68
Kissah; 91
Lazarus; 67, 79, 81
Lewis; 73
Lloyd; 105
Lucretia; 61, 65
Lucy; 60, 62
Margaret; 61
Mariah Joyner; 103
Martha; 60, 62-66
Mary; 59-65, 67-69, 81, 82
Matthew; 102, 103
Molly; 62
Nancy; 60, 62, 64, 83
Owen; 106
Paul; 1, 2, 3, 36, 45, 67, 79, 81, 93, 110
Penelope; 65, 66
Peter; 85, 86
Polly; 81, 82
Drake (cont.)
R. E., Jr.; 21, 22, 25, 31, 72, 73-76
Richard; 68, 69, 98, 99
Roy; 31
Rufus E.; 7, 11, 15, 21, 22, 39, 40, 71-73
Sally; 67, 80
Samuel; 13, 59-62, 65
Sarah; 64, 81
Sarah Kitchen; 47, 64, 79
Thadeus; 59
Thomas; 64, 65, 67-69, 82
Thomas Harrison; 7, 15, 50, 72, 85, 86
Thomazine; 68, 69
Timothy; 68
Tristam
William, 13, 47, 50, 64, 67, 80, 82, 99
Willie Thomas; 31
Winnefred; 62, 66
Zilla; 66
Dred Scott Decision (The); 107
Drew
Benjamin; 12
Duke of Gloucester Street; 104
Dunkley
John; 88
Dunning
Joyce Britt; 55
Dutch; 96
Dupree
Thomas; 44
Dysentery; 97

Eastern Shore; 97
Edmonds; 5
Edmunds (see Edmonds); 5
Edom (Va.); 107
Edwards; 27
Collin; 105
Jordan; 103
L. R.; 59
Martha; 47
Mary Hunt; 67
Newit; 64, 82
Peter; 85
Peterson; 85, 86
Robert; 67
Susan; 85, 86
William; 102
Eley; 5
Christian; 91
Robert; 91
Ellis
Ann; 47, 63
Ellsworth
Caroline; 47
Joseph; 105
Ellyson's Mill (Va.); 105
Ely (see Eley); 5
Emerson
John; 104
England
Church of; 60, 97, 98, 99
Country; 3, 95, 96-98, 110

English
Nathan; 44
Episcopal; 60, 98
Errata; 110
Erratum; 110
Evans
Benjamin, 90
Evands (see Evans); 43
Everett
Burwell; 33, 47
Caleb; 33
Charlotte; 33
Edward; 105
Exum; 27, 33, 35, 36, 46, 98, 99
Henry; 33
Jennet; 32
John; 33
Joseph; 31
Martha; 47
Mason; 33
Richard; 106
Samuel; 33
Sidney; 33, 34, 46
Simon; 31
Thomas; 33, 47, 106
Exum
Joseph

Faison
William; 50
Family History; 107
February
Edmond, Capt.; 88
Ferguson
Dixon; 45
Joseph; 106
Richard; 106
Fish Road; 35
Five Forks (Va.); 107
Forrest
Thomas; 95
Fort Fisher, N.C.; 8
Foster
Rebecca
Foushee
Nathan; 100
France; 96
Francis
Mary, 102
Nathaniel; 102
Salathial; 101
Sarah; 101
Franklin
City; 24, 71, 73
Frazier's Farm (Va.); 105
Fredericksburg; 90
French
James; 59

Gail (see Gale); 5
Gaines Mill (Va.); 105
Gale; 5
Gammon
David; 47
Gatling
Charity; 34, 56
Nancy Brett; 55
Sarah; 34
Garret
Edmond; 46
Mary Barnes; 46
Maria; 46
William; 46
Glendale (Va.); 105
Georgia; 11
Gettysburg (Penn.); 39, 71, 106
Gettysburg (movie); 107
Gillette
Joseph; 106
Gilliam
Robert
Godwin,
James; 87
Mills E.; 16
Good Friday Massacre; 95
Google Maps; 107
Grant
General; 15
Hugo;15-25
Richmond; 15, 17, 21
U. S., Gen.; 107
Gray
James; 102
Mills; 102
Robert; 105
Thomas; 91
William; 89
Great Awakening; 98
Great Britain; 98, 110
Great War (The); 74
Greenville County; 90
Greer
George Cabell; 11
Griffin
Ann; 67
Benjamin; 61
Everett; 106
John; 106
Mary Hunt Edwards; 67
Owen; 67
Grimmer
Robert; 89
William; 89
Grizzard
Hullen; 50
Jeremiah; 43
Guernsey; 71
Guil (see Gale); 5
Gurley
George; 60, 64, 84, 98, 99, 104, 105
Joseph; 98, 104
Mary; 60
Gwaltney; 10
Grimmer
Robert; 65

Haies (see Hayes); 5
Halley
William; 43
Harris
Charlotte; 99
John; 94
Martin; 88
William; 88, 89, 91
Harrisonburg (Va); 74, 107
Hart
Lyndon; 61
William; 58
Hartman
Annie; 75
Edna Dorothy; 74, 75
Emma; 75
Minnie; 75
Hase (see Hayes); 5
Hicksford (Emporia, Va.); 106
Hines
Patsy; 91
Sarah; 67, 81
Hayes; 5
Peter; 97
Head right system; 11, 96
Heritage Books; 79
Hertford (cow breed); 71
Hill
George; 97
Margaret Lucretia; 40
Hog killing; 22
Hollaman (see Holloman); 5
Holliman (see Holloman); 5
Holloman; 5
Holstein; 71
Hunt
Mary; 67
Huntsville (Ala.); 104
Hurricane Branch; 44

Illinois; 80
Indian; 96, 97
Massacre; 4, 95
International Harvester
Farmall B; 23
Irvin
L. M., Dr.; 88
Isle of Wight
County; 2-5, 9-11, 28, 57, 67, 68, 87, 88, 96-98, 110

Jackson
John; 80
James I, King; 95
James
Levinia; 43
Linney; 43
James Madison University; 74
James
River; 4, 95, 97, 110
Jamestown; 4, 68, 69, 95, 96, 97
Japan (Japanese); 76
Jarrell
Thomas; 87
Jersey; 71
Jerusalem
Virginia; 5
John Deere; 76
Johnson; 5
Hardy, 67
Robert; 88
Thomas; 45
Johnston (see Johnson); 5
Joiner (see Joyner) ; 5
Jones
James; 80, 89
Joseph; 87
Luten; 55
Molly; 89
Nathan; 105
Joyner, 5
Abraham; 44
Absolum; 67
Benjamin; 87
Bridge; 67, 68
Catherine; 88
Elizabeth; 87
James; 106
Mariah; 103
Thomas; 87, 88
Ulysses; 1
Joyner's Christian Church; 91

Kamikazes; 76
Kenchen (see Kitchen); 5
Kinchen
Elizabeth; 8s7
James; 87
Matthew; 87
Martha; 87
Patience; 87
Sarah; 87
Thomas; 87
William; 87
Kindred
Martha; 101
King
Martin Luther, Rev.; 24
Kirby's Creek; 44
Kitchen; 5
Ann; 89, 90
Benjamin; 89
Celia; 89
Collin; 89, 91, 106
Dixon; 89, 90
Elizabeth; 91
Enos; 90
Etheldred; 89-91
Frederick; 89
James; 88-90
Jesse; 89
John; 47, 88, 90
Julia; 90
Lucy; 89
Martha; 90, 91

Kitchen (cont.)
  Mary; 91
  Nancy; 90
  Nathan; 89, 90
  Patsy; 90
  Peggy; 90
  Rebecca; 90
  Robert; 88
  Sally; 89
  Samuel; 90
  Sarah; 47, 64, 80, 91
  Silvia; 89
  Thomas; 88-90
  William; 89-91
Kitchin
  John; 88
  Thomas; 88
Kitching
  Benjamin; 87
  Elizabeth; 89
  Etheldred; 87
  James; 87-89, 91
  Martha; 88
  Matthew; 89
  Thomas; 87
  Sarah; 87
  William; 89, 91
Knight
  Thomas; 102

Laydon
  Alice; 95
  John; 95
LaPorte
  Carol; 50, 51
Lee
  Linna; 30, 31, 45
  Robert E., Gen., 107
Leigh
  Joshua, Rev.; 21, 99
Lewis; 5
  Benjamin; 7
  Elizabeth; 7
  Fanny; 7
  Mary; 7
  Nanny; 7
  Sarah; 7
  Rebeccah; 7
  Zebulon; 7
Lightwood Swamp; 88
Liles
  Mary
Lilley
  Thomas; 87
Little
  Mr.; 74
Little Contenly Creek; 44
Little North Mountain; 74
London (England); 96
Longworth
  John; 88
Lotta (NC); 73
Louis (see Lewis); 5
Lower Parish; 97, 98
Lundy
  Byrd; 102
Lynchburg (Va.); 105

Maget; 5
Magette (see Maget); 5
Mahone
  Fielding; 61, 63
  William, Gen., 63
Malaria; 97
Malvern Hill (Va.) 105
Marine Corp; 76
Maryland; 11
Massey Harris; 23
McKinney
  Barnaby; 89
  Peggy Vaughan; 27, 30, 45
McMains
  Catherine; 46
  Jane; 46
Medford
  Patsy; 90
Meeting house; 36, 99
Meherrin River; 35, 58, 69
Memorial Day; 105
Merchant Marine; 75, 76
Methodist; 36, 98
  Archives; 30, 45
  Conference; 30, 99
  Ministers; 98-100
Mingo
  Lydia; 102
  Seth; 102
Mississippi; 99
Missouri; 11
Monroe
  Barbara Barnes; 5, 51
  Town of; 61
Moonshine(ing); 15, 39-41
Moore
  George; 97
  James; 91
  John; 102, 103
  Putnum; 101
  Sarah; 101
  Thomas; 97
Mountfort
  George; 59
Mt. Gilead, AME; 15, 17, 18, 21, 23, 25
Mt. Horeb Methodist Church; 45, 85, 99, 100
Mules; 74
Munger
  James; 43, 44, 50
  Michael; 43, 44
  Samuel; 43, 47
  William; 43
Murfree
  Simon; 99, 102
Murfree-Williams House; 104
Murfreesboro(NC); 35, 99
Murfreesboro Historical Association; 103, 104

Musgrove
    Charlotte Harris; 99
    Richard, Dr.; 99
Muster of 1624; 4, 95, 96

Nansemond County; 87, 88, 110
Navigation Acts; 96
Navy; 76
Nelson
    Margaret Van Ness; 27, 28, 30, 32, 43, 50, 51
New Hope Methodist Church; 100
New Jersey; 107
New Kent County; 97
New Market (Va.); 107
Newport News (Va.); 95
Newsom; 5
    James; 45, 49
    Newsom; 80
Newsome (see Newsom); 5
Newsoms (Va.); 73, 98, 100
    Elementary School; 74
    Post Office; 73
New World; 97
Nichol
    Bromfield; 61
Nuncupative will; 62
Norfolk, Va.; 7, 95
North America; 95
North Carolina; 10, 11, 27, 43, 50, 95, 97, 110
    Bertie County; 30, 34, 43, 45, 58, 95
    Chatham; 98
    Chowan County; 43, 57, 58, 69
    Edgecombe County; 11, 29, 43, 44, 49, 67, 79-81, 87
    Halifax; 43, 66, 98
    Hertford County; 11, 12, 34, 43, 47, 58, 69, 95
    Gates County; 30, 43, 45
    Johnston County; 11
    Martin; 43, 66
    Nash County; 11, 43, 66, 89
    Northampton County; 11, 29, 34, 43, 44, 46-50, 58, 66,87
    Perquimans County; 87
    Pitt County; 11, 29, 43, 43, 44, 47, 49, 65, 66
    Wake County; 11, 28
Northern Neck (Va.); 96
Northeast North Carolina; 55
Nottoway
    Chapel; 67, 68, 90, 91
    Parish; 28, 49, 59, 65, 84, 91, 97, 98
    River; 5, 61, 65, 81, 84, 85, 97
    Swamp; 45

O'Berry
    Henry; 45
Ohio; 11, 80
Old Point Comfort; 95
Olive Grove Methodist Church; 66
Oliver
    James; 47
    John; 52
    Joseph; 52
    Mary; 52
    Patience; 52
    Susan; 45
Oliver (cont.)
    Suzannah; 52
    William; 52
Orange (Va.)
    Circuit; 30

Pacific Ocean; 75
Parks
    Robert; 44
Parliament (English); 96
Parnell
    Jemima; 68
    Richard; 68
Parramore
    Thomas; 99, 100, 107
Pavlov
    Ivan; 71, 72
Penn
    William; 96
Pennsylvania; 40, 96, 107
Petersburg, Va.; 8, 3
Philips; 5
Phillips (see Philips); 5
Pierce
    William; 88
Piney Branch; 44
Piney Woods; 28, 73, 85
Pipkin
    Isaac; 104
    John; 104
Pipkin-Harrell- Chitty House
Point Lookout Prison (Md); 106
Pond
    Julia; 90
Pope
    Benjamin; 47, 49, 103
    Benjamin Evans; 27, 34, 35, 36, 43-47, 49
    Elizabeth; 35, 47
    Harrison; 47, 49
    Jonathan; 44
    Joseph; 35, 47, 49, 106
    Mary Vick, 49
    Mills; 102
    Sally; 35 , 47
    Sarah; 43, 44
    William; 102
Possum Branch; 40
Portsmouth, Va.; 7
Portsmouth Times; 102, 103
Powhatan Indians; 95
Pretlow
    Ann; 102, 103
    Sarah; 102, 103
Price
    Annie Hartman; 75
Primogenitor; 64
Putnam County (Ind.); 46, 81

Quakers; 4, 36, 87, 97, 103
Queen Ann; 110

Rae (see Rea); 5
Ray (see Rea); 5
Railey
  Benjamin; 50
  Richard (Dick); 19
  Russell; 19, 20, 22
Rea; 5
Reconstruction; 105
Records of Estates; 47
Reese
  Elizabeth; 101
  Joseph; 101
  Piety Vick; 101
Revel; 5
Revil (see Revel); 5
Reville (see Revel); 5
Revolution; 60, 95, 98, 98, 100
Richmond; 15, 27, 71, 99, 105, 106
Ridley
  Thomas; 100
Roanoke Rapids, N.C.; 7
Roberts-Vaughan Village Center; 104
Rochelle
  Clements; 62
  John
  Swamp Road; 35
Rockingham County; 74, 107
Rogers
  Sarah; 104
Rogerson Family; 87
Round Hill Swamp; 88
Royal Colony; 95
Ruffin
  Elizabeth; 87
  Robert; 87

Salem (Ma); 88
Sanders
  Bruce Phillips; 35
  Francis; 88
Sands (Va.); 73, 85
Sands Road; 29, 35
San Francisco (Cal); 75
Saurey
  Edward; 43
Savannah (Ga.); 91
Sawrey
  Edward; 50
Schuyler County (Ms); 100
Scotland; 60
Scott
  Ann; 102, 103
  Dred; 104, 107
  Etheldred; 104
  James Jordan; 102, 103
  John; 104
  Mary;104
  Miriam; 103
Scottish Parliament; 110
Seacock Swamp; 88
Sedley; 67
Senachwine Township (Ill.); 81
Seven Days; 39
Seven Pines; 39
Sharpe
  Robert; 89
Sharpsburg (Md).; 106
Sheepshead Bay (NY); 75
Sheiffield
  Josiah; 47
  Patience Oliver; 45, 47
Simes
  John; 88
Singer's Glenn; 75
Singer's Glenn Baptist Church; 74
Simmons
  Joseph; 32
  Olive Taylor; 32
Smith's Ferry; 65
Smith's Fort Plantation; 68
Smithfield
  Hams; 23
Snukes
  Daniel; 87
Spring Street; 15, 16
Spotsylvania Court House (Va.); 100, 106
Spotsylvania County; 107
Somerset, England; 68
Southampton; 46, 50, 55, 58, 69, 79-81, 84, 88, 89, 97, 98, 99, 100, 104, 105, 107, 110
  Cemetery Project; 35
  County; 2-5, 7-12, 20, 24, 27, 28
  Death register; 28, 30
  Deed Books; 55, 59, 80, 102, 103
  Historical Society; 27
  Insurrection; 100
  Land Tax Book; 30
  Marriage Register; 30, 32, 34, 55, 85, 98
  Minute Book; 110
  Order Book; 62, 102, 103
  Tax Lists; 56, 66
  Will Book; 32, 34, 35, 47, 102, 103
South Carolina; 11
Southeast Virginia; 55
South Petherton Parish, Somerset, England; 68
South Quay Baptist Church; 99
Starving Time; 95
Statesville Road; 35, 73
Stephenson; 15
St. Louis (Ms.); 104
St. Lukes
  Church; 98, 104
  Parish; 28, 49, 60, 61, 65, 81, 84, 85, 87, 97, 98
Story Station Road; 67
Suffolk, Va.; 7, 15, 16, 23
Sumner
  Byrd; 59, 60, 63
  Caroline; 59
  Mills; 59, 63
  Nancy; 59
Sunbeam; 45, 85
Sundie; 10
Surry
  County; 4, 68, 87, 88, 96, 97
Sussex(Va.) 89, 90
  Circuit; 30

Suter
Henry; 44

Tarlton
Mary; 88
Thomas; 88
Taylor
Charles; 61
Elizabeth; 61
Etheldred; 87
Henry; 100
Missouri Brett; 55
William; 87
Tennessee; 104
Terrapin Swamp; 87
Tharp (see Thorpe); 5
Tharpe (see Thorpe); 5
Thomas
George Henry, Gen.; 104, 105
Thorp (see Thorpe); 5
Thorpe; 5
Charity Barrett; 52
Edmond; 52
Joshua; 52
John; 52, 102
Tidewater
Region; 20
Tomlin
John; 106
Tory; 95
Travis
Ann; 91
Catherine; 90
Joseph; 101
Peggy; 90
Sarah; 101
Turkey Hunt; 72
Turner
Elizabeth Reese; 101
Kissah; 91
Nat; 100, 101
Samuel; 101
Sarah; 101
Tyler
Robert; 89

Ulithi Atoll; 76
Unification; 110
Upper Norfolk; 88
Upper Parish; 97
Upton
John; 11, 96

Vaughan
Ann; 102
George; 102
John; 104
Rebecca Foster; 102
Sarah Rogers; 104
Uriah; 104
William; 102
Velvin
Robert; 106

Vick
Archer; 31
Jesse; 44, 47
John; 103
Mary; 49
Newit; 49, 99
Piety; 101
Pilgrim; 46
Samuel; 44
Sela Barnes; 44
Shadrack; 43, 44
Vicksburg (Miss); 99
Vick's Old Church; 98
Virginia Advocate; 99
Virginia; 50, 81, 96, 107, 110
Commonwealth of; 7, 11, 27, 74
Library; 27
Penitentiary; 15, 19-21
Virginia Company; 95
Virginia Herald; 90

Waller
Levi; 102
Martha; 102
Martha Kindred; 102
War Between the States; 104
Ward
Rebecca; 66
Warrasquinoke; 11
Warren County, Ohio; 66, 98
Warrick Creek; 95
Washington
George; 40, 107
John; 90
William; 90
West
James; 47
Jesse; 47
West Virginia; 74, 107
Whiskey Rebellion; 40
White
Minnie Hartman; 75
Whitehead
Arthur; 46
Betsey; 46
Catherine; 101
John; 101
Margaret; 101
Martha; 101
Mary; 101
Minerva; 101
Mourning; 101
Richard; 101
Sally; 46
Whitfield
Phele; 80
Reuben; 45, 46, 80
Whitley
Benjamin; 105
John; 106

Wiggins
    Carr; 61
Wild Cat Swamp; 44
Wilderness (The), 107
Williams
    Benjamin; 67
    Eldridge; 105
    Elisha; 67
    Elizabeth; 67
    George; 102
    Mary; 67
    Micheal; 67
    Nancy Ann; 91
    Penelope; 67
    Simon; 67
    William; 67
Williamson
    Elijah; 99
    Francis; 88, 99
    James; 99
Williamsport (Md.); 106
Willoughby
    Thomas; 95
Wilson, Charles Morrow; 107
Wikipedia.com; 107
Winchester (Va.); 105
Wood
    Elizabeth; 61
Woodard
    Samuel; 27
    Wyatt Smith; 100
World War I; 74
World War II; 105
Worrell
    Benjamin; 46
    Elizabeth; 99
    Jesse; 106
    Joseph; 106
    Lewis; 46, 102
    Matilda; 46
    Richard; 46, 99
    Temperance; 46
Wright
    Job; 89, 91
    Mason; 89, 91
Wray (see Rea); 5

Yorktown (Va.); 66

1st North Carolina Infantry; 105, 106
2cd Corp, Army of Northern Virginia, 71
3rd Virginia Infantry; 105-107
5th Fleet, US Navy; 76
5th Virginia Calvary; 105
9th Virginia Infantry; 39, 106
12th Virginia Infantry; 100
13th Virginia Calvary; 106, 107
17th North Carolina Infantry; 8, 72
18th Virginia Artillery; 105, 106
32cd North Carolina Infantry; 71
41st Virginia Infantry; 105, 106

www.ingramcontent.com/pod-product-compliance
Lightning Source LLC
LaVergne TN
LVHW061248100826
845148LV00008B/1057